HAZE

21
DESIGNS
by Kim Hargreaves

CREDITS

DESIGN & STYLING
Kim Hargreaves

EDITOR
Kathleen Hargreaves

PHOTOGRAPHY
Nicole Jopeck

MODEL
Freya Haworth

HAIR & MAKE UP
Laura Howley

GRAPHIC DESIGN
Lyndsay Kaye

PATTERNS
Sue Whiting & Tricia McKenzie

First published in 2018 by Kim Hargreaves, 22 Broad Lane, Upperthong, Holmfirth, West Yorkshire, HD9 3JS, England.
printed by Lion FPG

British Library Cataloguing in Publication Data.
A catalogue record for this publication is availble from the British Library

ISBN -10   1-906487-32-4
ISBN -13   978-1-906487-32-4

CONTENTS

SOFT FOCUS

A collection with striking femininity
and effortless ease, take a journey
through the serene story and its
ever evolving colour palette, from
dusky tones & fluid silhouettes
that evoke an after dark elegance,
through to sweet shades of sherbet,
bonbon & candy that inject fizz,
froth & fun… whatever your mood
enjoy the allure of summer haze

DUSKY pretty sweater in an openwork fabric

LILA soft oversized cardigan with full sleeves

AUGUST crochet vest in subtle stripes & knitted edgings

REFLECT low-key button through sweater with side vents

STUNNING classic jacket with understated braids & cables

BEE chic crochet beret with subtle stripes

JULY crochet skirt with side lacing

GASP neat sweater in lattice & cables

STARTLE understated cardigan worked in two yarns

AMARA sweater worked in lattice & cables

WISTFUL neat cardigan with crochet trims

STRIKING close fitting vest in a slip stitch fabric

SUNSET understated reversible top

EXHALE fitted cardigan with sculpted cables

SIRAN neat chevron striped sweater

SIRAN neat chevron striped sweater

SUNRISE generous openwork sweater with cables

41

SWEET pretty reversible sweater with side vents

SUGAR understated sweater worked in two yarns

GLIMPSE pretty cardigan in an openwork fabric

BLUR off the shoulder sweater

DAZE relaxed raglan sweater in ombre stripes

SWEET pretty reversible sweater with side vents

LILA
EASY TO WEAR OVERSIZED CARDIGAN

	XS	S	M	L	XL	XXL
To fit bust	**81**	**86**	**91**	**97**	**102**	**109 cm**
	32	34	36	38	40	43 in

Rowan Softyak DK and Kidsilk Haze
Softyak DK
| | 8 | 9 | 9 | 10 | 10 | 11 x 50gm |
Kidsilk Haze
| | 5 | 6 | 6 | 6 | 7 | 7 x 25gm |
Photographed in Softyak DK in Shell and
Kidsilk Haze in Shadow

Needles
1 pair 4½mm (no 7) (US 7) needles
1 pair 5mm (no 6) (US 8) needles
1 pair 9mm (no 00) (US 13) needles

Tension
13 sts and 20 rows to 10 cm measured over
pattern using a combination of 4½mm
(US 7) and 9mm (US 13) needles and one
strand each of Softyak DK and Kidsilk Haze
held together.

Special note: We found it preferable to knit the
two yarns together from separate balls rather
than winding them together.

BACK
Cast on 76 (80: 84: 86: 90: 94) sts using
9mm (US 13) needles and one strand each of
Softyak DK and Kidsilk Haze held together.
Now work in patt as follows:
Row 1 (RS): Using a 4½mm (US 7) needle, knit.
Row 2: Using a 9mm (US 13) needle, purl.
These 2 rows form patt.
Cont in patt until back measures 73 (74: 75:
76: 77: 78) cm, ending with a WS row.
Shape shoulders
Keeping patt correct, cast off 5 (5: 6: 6: 6: 6) sts
at beg of next 6 (4: 6: 6: 6: 2) rows, then
– (6: -: -: -: 7) sts at beg of foll – (2: -: -: -: 4) rows.
46 (48: 48: 50: 54: 54) sts.
Shape back neck
Keeping patt correct, cont as follows:
Next row (RS): Cast off 6 (6: 6: 6: 7: 7) sts, K
until there are 10 (10: 10: 10: 11: 11) sts on
right needle and turn, leaving rem sts
on a holder.
Work each side of neck separately.
Cast off 4 sts at beg of next row.
Cast off rem 6 (6: 6: 6: 7: 7) sts.
With RS facing, rejoin yarns and cast off centre
14 (16: 16: 18: 18: 18) sts, K to end.
Complete to match first side, reversing
shapings.

LEFT FRONT
Cast on 41 (43: 45: 46: 48: 50) sts using
9mm (US 13) needles and one strand each of
Softyak DK and Kidsilk Haze held together.
Now work in patt as follows:
Row 1 (RS): Using a 4½mm (US 7) needle,
K to last st, pick up loop lying between needles
and place this loop on right needle (**Note:** This
loop does **NOT** count as a st), with yarn still at
back (WS) of work slip last st **purlwise**.
Row 2: Using a 9mm (US 13) needle, P tog the
first st and the picked-up loop, P to end.
Last 2 rows set the sts – slip st edging at front
opening edge of rows and all other sts in patt
as given for back.
Cont straight as now set until 68 (70: 70: 72:
72: 72) rows less have been worked than on
back to beg of shoulder shaping, ending with
a WS row.
Shape front slope
Keeping patt correct, cont as follows:

Next row (RS): K to last 7 sts, K2tog tbl, patt
5 sts.
Working all front slope decreases as set by last
row, dec 1 st at front opening edge of 6th (6th:
6th: 4th: 4th: 4th) and 0 (0: 0: 1: 1: 1) foll 4th
row, then on 7 (10: 10: 10: 10: 10) foll 6th
rows, then on 2 (0: 0: 0: 0: 0) foll 8th rows.
30 (31: 33: 33: 35: 37) sts.
Work 3 rows, ending with a WS row.
Shape shoulder
Keeping patt correct, cast off 5 (5: 6: 6: 6: 6) sts
at beg of next and foll 2 (1: 4: 2: 2: 0) alt rows,
then 6 (6: -: -: 7: 7) sts at beg of foll 2 (3: -: -:
2: 4) alt rows. 3 sts.
Inc 1 st at end of next row.
Cont as set on these 4 sts **only** (for back neck
border extension) until this strip measures
8 (9: 9: 10: 10: 10) cm, ending with a WS row.
Break yarn and leave these 4 sts on a holder.

RIGHT FRONT
Cast on 41 (43: 45: 46: 48: 50) sts using
9mm (US 13) needles and one strand each of
Softyak DK and Kidsilk Haze held together.
Now work in patt as follows:
Row 1 (WS): Using a 4½mm (US 7) needle, P
to last st, pick up loop lying between needles
and place this loop on right needle (**Note:**
This loop does **NOT** count as a st), slip last st
knitwise.
Row 2: Using a 9mm (US 13) needle, K tog **tbl**
the first st and the picked-up loop, K to end.
Last 2 rows set the sts – slip st edging at front
opening edge of rows and all other sts in patt.
Cont straight as now set until 68 (70: 70: 72:
72: 72) rows less have been worked than on
back to beg of shoulder shaping, ending with
a RS row.
Shape front slope
Keeping patt correct, cont as follows:
Next row (WS): P to last 7 sts, P2tog, patt 5 sts.
Working all front slope decreases as set by last
row, complete to match left front, reversing
shapings.

SLEEVES (both alike)
Main section
Cast on 52 (54: 56: 56: 58: 60) sts using
9mm (US 13) needles and one strand each of
Softyak DK and Kidsilk Haze held together.

Now work in patt as follows:

Row 1 (RS): Using a 4½mm (US 7) needle, knit.

Row 2: Using a 9mm (US 13) needle, purl.

These 2 rows form patt.

Keeping patt correct throughout, cont as follows:

Work 10 rows, ending with a WS row.

Next row (RS): K3, M1, K to last 3 sts, M1, K3.

Working all sleeve increases as set by last row, inc 1 st at each end of 14th (12th: 14th: 12th: 12th: 12th) and every foll 14th (12th: 16th: 12th: 12th: 14th) row to 60 (66: 66: 64: 64: 72) sts, then on every foll 16th (-: -: 14th: 14th: -) row until there are 62 (-: -: 68: 70: -) sts.

Cont straight until sleeve measures 40 (41: 42: 43: 44: 45) cm, ending with a WS row.

Shape top

Keeping patt correct , cast off 7 (8: 8: 8: 8: 9) sts at beg of next 2 rows, 7 (8: 8: 8: 9: 9) sts at beg of next 2 rows, then 8 (8: 8: 9: 9: 9) sts at beg of foll 2 rows.

Cast off rem 18 sts.

Cuff

With RS facing, using 5mm (US 8) needles and one strand each of Softyak DK and Kidsilk Haze held together, pick up and knit 34 (38: 38: 42: 42: 46) sts evenly along cast-on edge of main section.

Row 1 (WS): P2, *K2, P2, rep from * to end.

Row 2: K2, *P2, K2, rep from * to end.

These 2 rows form rib.

Cont in rib for a further 19 rows, ending with a WS row.

Cast off in rib.

MAKING UP

Press all pieces with a warm iron over a damp cloth.

Join both shoulder seams using back stitch or mattress stitch if preferred. Graft together both sets of 4 back neck border extension sts left on holders, then sew one edge to back neck. Mark points along side seam edges 25 (26: 26: 27: 28: 29) cm either side of shoulder seams, then sew shaped cast-off edges of sleeves to back and fronts between these points. Join side and sleeve seams.

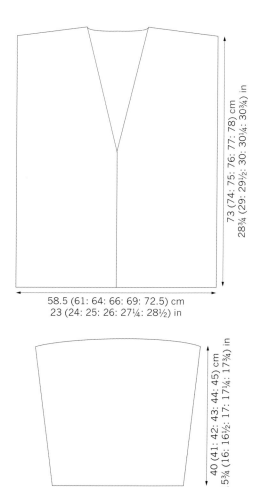

73 (74: 75: 76: 77: 78) cm
28¾ (29: 29½: 30: 30¼: 30¾) in

58.5 (61: 64: 66: 69: 72.5) cm
23 (24: 25: 26: 27¼: 28½) in

40 (41: 42: 43: 44: 45) cm
15¾ (16: 16½: 17: 17¼: 17¾) in

AUGUST

CROCHET VEST IN SUBTLE STRIPES WITH KNITTED EDGINGS

Recommendation ○○
Please see pages 12 & 13 for photographs.

	XS	S	M	L	XL	XXL	
To fit bust	**81**	**86**	**91**	**97**	**102**	**109**	cm
	32	34	36	38	40	43	in

Rowan Summerlite DK and Handknit Cotton
Summerlite DK
A Silvery Blue

	2	2	2	2	2	2	x 50gm

B Black

	2	2	2	2	2	2	x 50gm

C Steel

	2	2	2	2	2	2	x 50gm

D Mushroom

	1	1	2	2	2	2	x 50gm

E Mocha

	1	1	1	1	1	1	x 50gm

Handknit Cotton
F Black

	1	1	2	2	2	2	x 50gm

One-colour version
Summerlite DK

	6	6	6	7	7	7	x 50gm

Handknit Cotton

	1	1	1	1	1	1	x 50gm

Crochet hook and needles
3.50mm (no 9) (US E4) crochet hook
1 pair 3mm (no 11) (US 2/3) needles

Tension
18 sts and 15 rows to 10 cm measured over pattern using 3.50mm (US E4) crochet hook and Summerlite DK.

Crochet abbreviations
ch = chain; **dc** = double crochet; **htr** = half treble; **ss** = slip stitch.

One-colour version
Work as given for multi-colour version but using same colour throughout.

STRIPE SEQUENCE
Rows 1 and 2: Using yarn A.
Rows 3 and 4: Using yarn B.
Row 5: Using yarn E.
Rows 6 and 7: Using yarn C.
Rows 8 and 9: Using yarn D.
Rows 10 and 11: Using yarn A.
Rows 12 and 13: Using yarn B.
Row 14: Using yarn C.
Rows 15 and 16: Using yarn A.
Rows 17 and 18: Using yarn E.
Rows 19 and 20: Using yarn D.
Row 21: Using yarn C.
Row 22: Using yarn B.
Row 23: Using yarn A.
Row 24: Using yarn D.
Rows 25 and 26: Using yarn C.
Row 27: Using yarn A.
Rows 28 and 29: Using yarn B.
Rows 30 and 31: Using yarn C.
Row 32: Using yarn E.
Row 33: Using yarn A.
Rows 34 to 36: Using yarn D.
Rows 37 and 38: Using yarn B.
Row 39: Using yarn C.
Row 40: Using yarn B.
Rows 41 to 43: Using yarn A.
Rows 44 to 46: Using yarn C.
Row 47: Using yarn D.
These 47 rows form stripe sequence and are repeated.

BACK
Make 71 (75: 79: 85: 89: 95) ch using 3.50mm (US E4) crochet hook and yarn A.
Row 1 (WS): 1 dc into 2nd ch from hook, 1 dc into each ch to end, turn. 70 (74: 78: 84: 88: 94) sts.
Row 2: 2 ch (counts as first htr), miss dc at base of 2 ch, 1 htr into each dc to end, turn.
Now work in patt as follows:
Row 3: 2 ch (counts as first htr), miss htr at base of 2 ch, 1 htr into each htr to end, working last htr into top of 2 ch at beg of previous row, turn.
Last row forms patt, and last 2 rows form stripe sequence rows 1 and 2 (see above).

Joining in and breaking off colours as required and beg with stripe sequence row 3, cont in patt and stripe sequence as now set throughout as follows:
Cont straight until back measures 37 (37: 38: 38: 38: 38) cm, ending with a WS row.
Shape armholes
Next row (RS): Ss across and into 6th st, 2 ch (counts as first htr), miss st at base of 2 ch, 1 htr into each htr to last 5 sts and turn, leaving rem 5 sts unworked.
60 (64: 68: 74: 78: 84) sts.
Sizes XS, M, L, XL and XXL only
Next row: 2 ch (counts as first htr), miss st at base of 2 ch, 1 htr into each of next 2 htr, miss 1 htr, 1 htr into next htr, miss 1 htr, 1 htr into each st to last 6 sts, miss 1 htr, 1 htr into next htr, miss 1 htr, 1 htr into each of last 3 sts, turn.
Rep last row 0 (-: 1: 1: 1: 4) times more.
56 (-: 60: 66: 70: 64) sts.
All sizes
Next row: 2 ch (counts as first htr), miss st at base of 2 ch, 1 htr into each of next 2 htr, miss 1 htr, 1 htr into each st to last 4 sts, miss 1 htr, 1 htr into each of last 3 sts, turn.**
Rep last row 19 (22: 20: 22: 24: 21) times more, ending with a WS row.
16 (18: 18: 20: 20: 20) sts.
Fasten off.

FRONT
Work as for back to **.
Rep last row 11 (14: 12: 14: 16: 13) times more, ending with a WS row.
32 (34: 34: 36: 36: 36) sts.
Shape front neck
Keeping stripes correct, cont as follows:
Next row (RS): 2 ch (counts as first htr), miss st at base of 2 ch, 1 htr into each of next 2 htr, miss 1 htr, 1 htr into each of next 5 htr and turn, leaving rem sts unworked. 8 sts.
Work each side of neck separately.
Next row: Ss across and into 2nd st, 2 ch (counts as first htr), miss st at base of 2 ch, 1 htr into each of next 2 htr, miss 1 htr, 1 htr into each of last 3 sts, turn. 6 sts.
Next row: 2 ch (counts as first htr), miss st at base of 2 ch, 1 htr into each of next 2 htr, miss 1 htr, 1 htr into next htr and turn, leaving rem st unworked. 4 sts.

Next row: Ss across and into 2nd st, 2 ch (counts as first htr), miss st at base of 2 ch and next htr, 1 htr into last st. 2 sts.
Fasten off.
Return to last complete row worked, miss next 14 (16: 16: 18: 18: 18) sts, rejoin appropriate yarn to next st, 2 ch (counts as first htr), miss st where yarn was rejoined, 1 htr into each of next 4 htr, miss 1 htr, 1 htr into each of last 3 sts, turn. 8 sts.
Complete to match first side, reversing shapings.

MAKING UP
Press all pieces with a warm iron over a damp cloth.
Using back stitch or mattress stitch if preferred, join both side seams.

Left armhole border
With RS facing, using 3mm (US 2/3) needles and yarn F, pick up and knit 45 (47: 50: 53: 57: 62) sts down left back armhole edge from top of last row to side seam, 1 st from top of side seam, and 41 (43: 46: 49: 53: 58) sts up left front armhole edge to fasten-off point. 87 (91: 97: 103: 111: 121) sts.
Row 1 (WS): K1, *P1, K1, rep from * to end.
Row 2: *P1, K1 tbl, rep from * to last st, inc in last st.
Last 2 rows form rib and start shaping.
Work in rib for a further 7 (7: 7: 9: 9: 9) rows, inc 1 st at end of 2nd and foll 2 (2: 2: 3: 3: 3) alt rows, taking inc sts into rib and ending with a WS row.
Cast off all 91 (95: 101: 109: 117: 127) sts in rib.

Right armhole border
With RS facing, using 3mm (US 2/3) needles and yarn F, pick up and knit 41 (43: 46: 49: 53: 58) sts down right front armhole edge from fasten-off point to side seam, 1 st from top of side seam, and 45 (47: 50: 53: 57: 62) sts up right back armhole edge to top of last row. 87 (91: 97: 103: 111: 121) sts.
Row 1 (WS): K1, *P1, K1, rep from * to end.
Row 2: Inc in first st, *K1 tbl, P1, rep from * to end.
Last 2 rows form rib and start shaping.
Work in rib for a further 7 (7: 7: 9: 9: 9) rows, inc 1 st at beg of 2nd and foll 2 (2: 2: 3: 3: 3) alt rows, taking inc sts into rib and ending with a WS row.
Cast off all 91 (95: 101: 109: 117: 127) sts in rib.

Neckband and shoulder straps
Cast on 43 sts using 3mm (US 2/3) needles and yarn F – these sts will form right shoulder strap.
Break yarn and leave these sts on a holder.
Cast on 43 sts using 3mm (US 2/3) needles and yarn F – these sts will form left shoulder strap.
Now, with RS facing, work across 43 left shoulder strap sts as follows: P1, (K1 tbl, P1) 21 times, pick up and knit 9 sts down row-end edge of left armhole border, 6 sts down left side of front neck, 17 (19: 19: 21: 21: 21) sts from front, 6 sts up right side of front neck, and 9 sts up row-end edge of right armhole border, now work across 43 sts on right shoulder strap holder as follows: P1, (K1 tbl, P1) 21 times, pick up and knit 9 sts along back row-end edge of right armhole border, 20 (22: 22: 24: 24: 24) sts from back, and 9 sts along back row-end edge of left armhole border.
171 (175: 175: 179: 179: 179) sts.
Row 1 (WS): K1, *P1, K1, rep from * to end.
Row 2: P1, *K1 tbl, P1, rep from * to end.
Last 2 rows form rib.
Work in rib for a further 5 (5: 5: 7: 7: 7) rows, ending with a WS row.
Cast off in rib.
Join row-end edges of neckband and left shoulder strap.

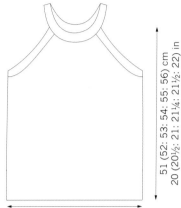

51 (52: 53: 54: 55: 56) cm
20 (20½: 21: 21¼: 21½: 22) in

39 (41: 43.5: 46.5: 49: 52) cm
15¼ (16¼: 17¼: 18¼: 19¼: 20½) in

STRIKING
CLOSE FITTING VEST IN A SLIP STITCH FABRIC

	XS	S	M	L	XL	XXL
To fit bust	**81**	**86**	**91**	**97**	**102**	**109 cm**
	32	34	36	38	40	43 in

Rowan Cotton Glacé

6　6　7　7　8　8　x 50gm

Photographed in Black

Needles
1 pair 2¾mm (no 12) (US 2) needles
1 pair 3¼mm (no 10) (US 3) needles

Extras – 75 cm of 2.5 cm wide ribbon (for shoulder straps)

Tension
28 sts and 38 rows to 10 cm measured over main pattern using 3¼mm (US 3) needles.

BACK and FRONT (both alike)
Cast on 107 (113: 121: 127: 135: 145) sts using 2¾mm (US 2) needles.
Working **all** slipped sts purlwise with yarn at **WS** of work (this is **back** of work on RS rows), cont as follows:
Row 1 (RS): K3 (1: 5: 3: 2: 2), sl 1, *K4, sl 1, rep from * to last 3 (1: 5: 3: 2: 2) sts, K3 (1: 5: 3: 2: 2).
Row 2: K3 (1: 5: 3: 2: 2), P1, *K4, P1, rep from * to last 3 (1: 5: 3: 2: 2) sts, K3 (1: 5: 3: 2: 2).
These 2 rows form border patt.
Work in border patt for a further 16 rows, ending with a WS row.
Change to 3¼mm (US 3) needles.
Now work in main patt as follows:
Row 1 (RS): P3 (1: 5: 3: 2: 2), sl 1, *P4, sl 1, rep from * to last 3 (1: 5: 3: 2: 2) sts, P3 (1: 5: 3: 2: 2).
Row 2: K3 (1: 5: 3: 2: 2), P1, *K4, P1, rep from * to last 3 (1: 5: 3: 2: 2) sts, K3 (1: 5: 3: 2: 2).
These 2 rows form patt.
Keeping patt correct throughout, cont as follows:
Work 9 (9: 11: 11: 11: 11) rows, ending with a **RS** row.
Next row (WS): Patt 9 (7: 11: 9: 8: 8) sts, K2tog, patt to last 11 (9: 13: 11: 10: 10) sts, K2tog tbl, patt 9 (7: 11: 9: 8: 8) sts.
Work 7 rows.
Rep last 8 rows twice more.
101 (107: 115: 121: 129: 139) sts.
Next row (WS): Patt 11 (9: 13: 11: 10: 10) sts, K2tog, patt to last 13 (11: 15: 13: 12: 12) sts, K2tog tbl, patt 11 (9: 13: 11: 10: 10) sts.
Work 7 rows.
Rep last 8 rows once more, then first of these rows (the dec row) again.
95 (101: 109: 115: 123: 133) sts.
Work 13 rows, ending with a **RS** row.
Next row (WS): Patt 11 (9: 13: 11: 10: 10) sts, M1, patt to last 11 (9: 13: 11: 10: 10) sts, M1, patt 11 (9: 13: 11: 10: 10) sts.
Work 7 rows.
Rep last 8 rows twice more.
101 (107: 115: 121: 129: 139) sts.
Next row (WS): Patt 9 (7: 11: 9: 8: 8) sts, M1, patt to last 9 (7: 11: 9: 8: 8) sts, M1, patt 9 (7: 11: 9: 8: 8) sts.
Work 7 rows.
Rep last 8 rows once more, then first of these rows (the inc row) again.
107 (113: 121: 127: 135: 145) sts.

Cont straight until work measures 33 (33: 34: 34: 34: 34) cm, ending with a WS row.
Shape armholes
Keeping patt correct, cast off 6 (4: 8: 11: 10: 15) sts at beg of next 2 rows.
95 (105: 105: 105: 115: 115) sts.
Next row (RS): Patt 4 sts, P2tog, patt to last 6 sts, P2tog tbl, patt 4 sts.
Working all decreases as set by last row, dec 1 st at each end of 2nd and foll 12 (18: 18: 14: 22: 20) alt rows, then on 4 (2: 2: 5: 2: 4) foll 4th rows.
59 (61: 61: 63: 63: 63) sts.
Work 3 rows, ending with a WS row.
Change to 2¾mm (US 2) needles.
Next row (RS): P2, sl 1, K1, K2tog, K3 (4: 4: 0: 0: 0), sl 1, *K4, sl 1, rep from * to last 9 (10:10: 6: 6: 6) sts, K3 (4: 4: 0: 0: 0), K2tog tbl, K1, sl 1, P2.
Next row: K2, sl 1, K5 (6: 6: 2: 2: 2), sl 1, *K4, sl 1, rep from * to last 8 (9: 9: 5: 5: 5) sts, K5 (6: 6: 2: 2: 2), sl 1, K2.
Last 2 rows set position of border patt as given for cast-on edge.
Now working all decreases as set by first of last 2 rows, cont in border patt, dec 1 st at each end of 3rd and foll 6th row. 53 (55: 55: 57: 57: 57) sts.
Work 4 rows, ending with a **RS** row.
Cast off **all** sts knitwise (on **WS**).

MAKING UP
Press pieces with a warm iron over a damp cloth.
Using back stitch or mattress stitch if preferred, join both side seams.
Cut ribbon into 2 equal lengths. Attach one end of each piece to inside of upper edge of front. Adjust length of shoulder straps and then attach other end of each piece to inside of upper edge of back.

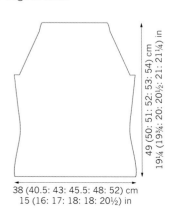

49 (50: 51: 52: 53: 54) cm
19¼ (19¾: 20: 20½: 21: 21¼) in

38 (40.5: 43: 45.5: 48: 52) cm
15 (16: 17: 18: 18: 20½) in

JULY

CROCHET SKIRT WITH SIDE LACING

Recommendation ○○
Please see pages 20 & 21 for photographs.

	XS	S	M	L	XL	XXL
To fit bust	**81**	**86**	**91**	**97**	**102**	**109 cm**
	32	34	36	38	40	43 in

Rowan Handknit Cotton

9	10	11	12	13	14	x 50gm

Photographed in Black

Crochet hooks
3.50mm (no 9) (US E4) crochet hook
4.00mm (no 8) (US G6) crochet hook

Side lacing – purchased or crochet ties 120cm long

Tension
18 sts and 12 rows to 10 cm measured over yoke pattern using 3.50mm (US E4) crochet hook.

Crochet abbreviations
ch = chain; **dc** = double crochet; **sp(s)** = space(s); **tr** = treble.

FRONT YOKE (worked downwards)
Make 55 (59: 63: 67: 73: 81) ch using 3.50mm (US E4) crochet hook.
Row 1 (RS): 1 tr into 4th ch from hook, 1 tr into each ch to end, turn.
53 (57: 61: 65: 71: 79) sts.
Row 2: 3 ch (counts as first tr), miss st at base of 3 ch, 1 tr into each st to end, working last tr into top of 3 ch at beg of previous row, turn. This row forms patt.
Keeping patt correct, cont as follows:
Row 3: 3 ch (counts as first tr), miss st at base of 3 ch, 1 tr into each of next 5 sts, *2 tr into next st, 1 tr into each of next 3 sts, 2 tr into next st*, 1 tr into each st to last 11 sts, rep from * to * once more, 1 tr into each of last
6 sts, turn.
57 (61: 65: 69: 75: 83) sts.
Work 1 row, then rep row 3.
61 (65: 69: 73: 79: 87) sts.
Work 1 (1: 1: 1: 3: 3) rows, then rep row 3 again. 65 (69: 73: 77: 83: 91) sts.
Work 1 (1: 1: 1: 3: 3) rows.
Next row: 3 ch (counts as first tr), miss st at base of 3 ch, 1 tr into each of next 5 sts, 2 tr into next st, 1 tr into each st to last 7 sts, 2 tr into next st, 1 tr into each of last 6 sts, turn.
67 (71: 75: 79: 85: 93) sts.
Next row: 3 ch (counts as first tr), miss st at base of 3 ch, 1 tr into each of next 5 sts, *1 ch, miss 1 st, 1 tr into next st, rep from * to last 5 sts, 1 tr into each of last 5 sts, turn.
Next row: 3 ch (counts as first tr), miss st at base of 3 ch, 1 tr into each st and ch sp to end, working last tr into top of 3 ch at beg of previous row, turn.**
Rep last 2 rows once more, inc 4 (6: 2: 4: 4: 2) sts evenly across 2nd of these rows. 71 (77: 77: 83: 89: 95) sts.
Fasten off.

BACK YOKE (worked downwards)
Work as given for front yoke to **.
Rep last 2 rows once more, inc 6 (8: 4: 6: 6: 4) sts evenly across 2nd of these rows.
73 (79: 79: 85: 91: 97) sts.
Fasten off.
Place marker on centre st of last row.

SKIRT SECTION (worked downwards)
Join yoke section along row-end edges of last row (to form side seams below laced side seam openings).
With RS facing and using 4.00mm (US G6) crochet hook, attach yarn to st 2 sts **before** marked centre back st and, working into each st of last rows of yoke sections, work around lower edge of joined yoke sections as follows:
Next round (RS): 1 ch (does NOT count as st), 1 dc into st at base of 1 ch, *5 ch, miss 3 sts (for first rep, this is marked centre back st and one st each side), 1 dc into next st, rep from * to last 3 sts, 2 ch, miss 3 sts, 1 tr into first dc, do NOT turn. 36 (39: 39: 42: 45: 48) ch sps.
Now work in patt as follows:
Round 1 (RS): 1 ch (does NOT count as st), 1 dc into ch sp partly formed by tr at end of previous round, *7 tr into next ch sp, 1 dc into next ch sp**, 5 ch, 1 dc into next ch sp, rep from * to end, ending last rep at **, 2 ch, 1 tr into first dc, turn.
12 (13: 13: 14: 15: 16) patt reps.

70 (72: 72: 74: 74: 76) cm
27½ (28½: 28½: 29: 29: 30) in

40.5 (43: 44.5: 46.5: 49: 53.5) cm
16 (17: 17½: 18½: 19½: 21) in

Continued on next page…

DUSKY

PRETTY SWEATER IN AN OPENWORK FABRIC

Recommendation ○○
Please see pages 8 & 9 for photographs.

	XS	S	M	L	XL	XXL	
To fit bust	**81**	**86**	**91**	**97**	**102**	**109**	**cm**
	32	34	36	38	40	43	in

Rowan Summerlite DK

| | 7 | 7 | 8 | 8 | 9 | 10 | x50g |

Photographed in Black

Needles
1 pair 2¾mm (no 12) (US 2) needles
1 pair 3¼mm (no 10) (US 3) needles

Buttons - 4

Tension
26 sts and 52 rows to 10 cm measured over garter stitch using 2¾mm (US 2) needles. 16 sts and 36 rows to 10 cm measured over main pattern using 3¼mm (US 3) needles.

BACK

Cast on 104 (110: 118: 124: 130: 140) sts using 2¾mm (US 2) needles.
Work in g st for 14 rows, ending with a WS row.
Now work in lower patt as follows:
Row 1 (RS): Knit.
Row 2: K7, yfrn, P2tog, *yrn, P2tog, rep from * to last 7 sts, K7.
Rows 3 and 4: As row 2.
Rows 5 to 10: Knit.
Last 10 rows form lower patt.
Work in lower patt for a further 40 rows, ending with a WS row.
Place markers at both ends of last row (to denote top of side seam openings).
Change to 3¼mm (US 3) needles.**
Next row (RS): K4 (5: 4: 4: 5: 5), (K2tog, K1, K2tog) 19 (20: 22: 23: 24: 26) times, K5 (5: 4: 5: 5: 5). 66 (70: 74: 78: 82: 88) sts.
Now work in main patt as follows:
Row 1 (WS): P1 (1: 1: 1: 1: 2), *yrn, P2tog, rep from * to last 1 (1: 1: 1: 1: 2) sts, P1 (1: 1: 1: 1: 2).
Row 2: As row 1.
These 2 rows form main patt.
Cont in main patt until back measures 37 (37: 38: 38: 38: 38) cm, ending with a WS row.
Shape armholes
Keeping patt correct, cast off 4 (4: 4: 4: 4: 5) sts at beg of next 2 rows.
58 (62: 66: 70: 74: 78) sts.

Dec **2** sts at each end of next and foll 0 (0: 1: 1: 2: 2) alt rows, then on 0 (1: 1: 1: 1: 1) foll 4th row. 54 (54: 54: 58: 58: 62) sts.
Cont straight until armhole measures 18 (19: 19: 20: 21: 22) cm, ending with a WS row.
Shape shoulders and back neck
Next row (RS): Cast off 4 sts, patt until there are 8 (8: 8: 8: 8: 10) sts on right needle and turn, leaving rem sts on a holder.
Work each side of neck separately.
Cast off 4 sts at beg of next row.
Cast off rem 4 (4: 4: 4: 4: 6) sts.
With RS facing, rejoin yarn and cast off centre 30 (30: 30: 34: 34: 34) sts, patt to end.
Complete to match first side, reversing shapings.

FRONT

Work as given for back to **.
Next row (RS): K5 (6: 5: 5: 6: 6), (K2tog, K1) 1 (0: 0: 1: 0: 0) times, (K2tog, K1, K2tog) 8 (9: 10: 10: 11: 12) times, K8, (K2tog, K1, K2tog) 8 (9: 10: 10: 11: 12) times, (K1, K2tog) 1 (0: 0: 1: 0: 0) times, K5 (6: 5: 5: 6: 6).
70 (74: 78: 82: 86: 92) sts.
Now work in patt as follows:
Row 1 (WS): P1 (1: 1: 1: 1: 2), (yrn, P2tog) 15 (16: 17: 18: 19: 20) times, K8, (yrn, P2tog) 15 (16: 17: 18: 19: 20) times, P1 (1: 1: 1: 1: 2).
Row 2: As row 1.

JULY – *Continued from previous page.*

Round 2: 1 ch (does NOT count as st), 1 dc into ch sp partly formed by tr at end of previous round, *5 ch, miss (1 dc and 1 tr), 1 dc into next tr, 5 ch, miss 3 tr, 1 dc into next tr**, 5 ch, miss (1 tr and 1 dc), 1 dc into next ch sp, rep from * to end, ending last rep at **, 2 ch, 1 tr into first dc, turn.
Last 2 rounds form patt.
Cont in patt until skirt measures 70 (72: 72: 74: 74: 76) cm from upper edge of yoke section, ending after patt round 1.
Fasten off.

MAKING UP
Press all pieces with a warm iron over a damp cloth.
Optional crochet side ties (make 2)
Using 3.50mm (US E4) crochet hook, make a length of ch approx 120 cm long and fasten off.
Using photograph as a guide and threading ties between sts of yoke sections, thread ties in and out of side seam edges to lace up side seams openings.

These 2 rows set the sts – centre front 8 sts in g st with all other sts in main patt.

Cont as now set until 58 rows less have been worked than on back to start of armhole shaping, ending with a WS row.

Divide for front opening
Next row (RS): Patt 31 (33: 35: 37: 39: 42) sts and turn, leaving rem sts on a holder.

Work each side of front separately.

Next row (WS): Cast on and K 8 sts, patt to end. 39 (41: 43: 45: 47: 50) sts.

Keeping sts correct as set by last row (with front opening edge 8 sts in g st and all other sts in patt), cont as follows:

Work 54 rows, ending with a WS row.

Shape front neck
Next row (RS): Patt 24 (26: 28: 30: 32: 35) sts and turn, leaving rem 15 sts on a holder (for neckband).

Work 1 row, ending with a WS row.

Shape armhole
Keeping patt correct, cast off 4 (4: 4: 4: 4: 5) sts at beg and dec 2 sts at end of next row. 18 (20: 22: 24: 26: 28) sts.

Work 1 row.

Dec **2** sts at neck edge of 4th and 1 (1: 1: 2: 2: 2) foll 6th rows, then on foll 8th row, then on foll 12th row **and at same time** dec **2** sts at armhole edge of next and foll 0 (0: 1: 1: 2: 2) alt rows, then on 0 (1: 1: 1: 1: 1) foll 4th row. 8 (8: 8: 8: 8: 10) sts.

Cont straight until front matches back to start of shoulder shaping, ending with a WS row.

Shape shoulder
Cast off 4 sts at beg of next row.

Work 1 row.

Cast off rem 4 (4: 4: 4: 4: 6) sts.

With RS facing, rejoin yarn at base of front opening, K8, patt to end. 39 (41: 43: 45: 47: 50) sts.

Keeping sts correct as set, work 9 rows, ending with a WS row.

Next row (RS): K3, K2tog, yfwd (to make a buttonhole), K3, patt to end.

Making a further 2 buttonholes in this way on 2 foll 16th rows, complete to match first side, reversing shapings and working first row of front neck shaping as follows:

Shape front neck
Next row (RS): K15 and slip these sts onto a holder (for neckband), patt to end. 24 (26: 28: 30: 32: 35) sts.

SLEEVES (both alike)
Cast on 72 (76: 76: 80: 82: 86) sts using 2¾mm (US 2) needles.

Work in g st for 14 rows, ending with a WS row.

Now work in lower patt as follows:

Row 1 (RS): Knit.

Row 2: P1, *yrn, P2tog, rep from * to last st, P1.

Rows 3 and 4: As row 2.

Rows 5 to 10: Knit.

Last 10 rows complete lower patt.

Change to 3¼mm (US 3) needles.

Next row (RS): K3 (3: 3: 2: 3: 3), (K2tog, K1, K2tog) 13 (14: 14: 15: 15: 16) times, K4 (3: 3: 3: 4: 3). 46 (48: 48: 50: 52: 54) sts.

Now work in main patt as follows:

Row 1 (WS): P1, *yrn, P2tog, rep from * to last st, P1.

Row 2: As row 1.

These 2 rows form main patt.

Work in patt for a further 15 rows, ending with a WS row.

Next row (RS): Inc **twice** in first st (by working into front, back and front again), patt to last st, inc **twice** in last st. 50 (52: 52: 54: 56: 58) sts.

Size XXL only
Inc 1 st at each end of foll 12th row. 60 sts.

All sizes
Cont straight until sleeve measures 13 (14: 14: 15: 16: 17) cm, ending with a WS row.

Shape top
Keeping patt correct, cast off 4 (4: 4: 4: 4: 5) sts at beg of next 2 rows.

42 (44: 44: 46: 48: 50) sts.

Dec **2** sts at each end of 3rd (5th: 5th: 5th: 7th: 7th) and 0 (0: 0: 0: 1: 2) foll 12th rows, then on 2 (2: 2: 3: 1: 0) foll 10th rows, then on 1 (1: 1: 0: 1: 1) foll 8th row, then on 2 foll 4th rows. 18 (20: 20: 22: 24: 26) sts.

Work 1 row, ending with a WS row.

Cast off **loosely**.

MAKING UP
Press all pieces with a warm iron over a damp cloth.

Join both shoulder seams using back stitch or mattress stitch if preferred.

Neckband
With RS facing and using 2¾mm (US 2) needles, slip 15 sts from right front holder onto right needle, rejoin yarn and pick up and knit 35 (38: 38: 41: 43: 46) sts up right side of front neck, 42 (42: 42: 45: 45: 45) sts from back, and 35 (38: 38: 41: 43: 46) sts down left side of front neck, then K across 15 sts on left front holder.

142 (148: 148: 157: 161: 167) sts.

Next row (WS): Knit.

Next row: K3, K2tog, yfwd (to make 4th buttonhole), K to end.

Work in g st for a further 10 rows, ending with a RS row.

Cast off knitwise (on **WS**).

Neatly sew cast-on edge at base of left front opening edge in place behind right front opening edge. Join side seams, leaving side seams open below markers (for side seam slit openings). Join sleeve seams. Insert sleeves into armholes. Sew on buttons.

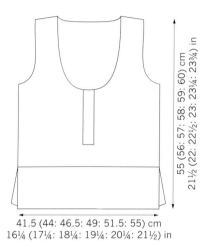

41.5 (44: 46.5: 49: 51.5: 55) cm
16¼ (17¼: 18¼: 19¼: 20¼: 21½) in

55 (56: 57: 58: 59: 60) cm
21½ (22: 22½: 23: 23¼: 23¾) in

13 (14: 14: 15: 16: 17) cm
5 (5½: 5½: 6: 6¼: 6¾) in

Recommendation ○○
Please see pages 14 & 15 for photographs.

	XS	S	M	L	XL	XXL	
To fit bust	**81**	**86**	**91**	**97**	**102**	**109**	**cm**
	32	34	36	38	40	43	in

Rowan Summerlite DK

| 8 | 8 | 9 | 9 | 10 | 11 | x 50gm |

Photographed in Mocha

Needles
1 pair 2¾mm (no 12) (US 2) needles
1 pair 3¼mm (no 10) (US 3) needles

Buttons - 3

Tension
24 sts and 34 rows to 10 cm measured over stocking stitch using 3¼mm (US 3) needles.

REFLECT
LOW-KEY BUTTON THROUGH SWEATER WITH SIDE VENTS

BACK
Cast on 97 (103: 109: 115: 121: 131) sts using 2¾mm (US 2) needles.
Work in g st for 14 rows, ending with a WS row.
Change to 3¼mm (US 3) needles.
Next row (RS): Knit.
Next row: K8, P to last 8 sts, K8.
Last 2 rows set the sts – 8 sts in g st at each end of rows with all other sts in st st.
Keeping sts correct as now set, cont as follows:
Work 14 (14: 16: 16: 16: 16) rows, ending with a WS row.
Next row (RS): K9, K2tog, K to last 11 sts, K2tog tbl, K9.
Working all side seam decreases as set by last row, cont as follows:
Dec 1 st at each end of 8th row.
93 (99: 105: 111: 117: 127) sts.
Work 1 row, ending with a WS row.
Place markers at both ends of last row (to denote top of side seam openings).
Now working **all** sts in st st, cont as follows:
Dec 1 st at each end of 7th and foll 8th row.
89 (95: 101: 107: 113: 123) sts.**
Work 17 (17: 19: 19: 19: 19) rows, ending with a WS row.
Next row (RS): K3, M1, K to last 3 sts, M1, K3.
Working all side seam increases as set by last row, inc 1 st at each end of 14th and 2 foll 14th rows.
97 (103: 109: 115: 121: 131) sts.
Work 13 rows, ending with a WS row.
(Back should measure approx 37 (37: 38: 38: 38: 38) cm.)
Shape armholes
Cast off 4 (4: 5: 5: 6: 6) sts at beg of next 2 rows.
89 (95: 99: 105: 109: 119) sts.
Dec 1 st at each end of next 3 (5: 5: 7: 7: 9) rows, then on foll 3 (3: 4: 4: 4: 6) alt rows, then on foll 4th row.
75 (77: 79: 81: 85: 87) sts.
Cont straight until armhole measures 18 (19: 19: 20: 21: 22) cm, ending with a WS row.
Shape shoulders and back neck
Next row (RS): Cast off 7 (7: 7: 7: 8: 8) sts, K until there are 15 (15: 16: 16: 17: 18) sts on right needle and turn, leaving rem sts on a holder.
Work each side of neck separately.

Dec 1 st at neck edge of next 2 rows **and at same time** cast off 7 (7: 7: 7: 8: 8) sts at beg of 2nd row.
Work 1 row.
Cast off rem 6 (6: 7: 7: 7: 8) sts.
With RS facing, rejoin yarn and cast off centre 31 (33: 33: 35: 35: 35) sts, K to end.
Complete to match first side, reversing shapings.

FRONT
Work as given for back to **.
Work 16 (16: 18: 18: 18: 18) rows, ending with a **RS** row.
Divide for front opening
Next row (WS): P40 (43: 46: 49: 52: 57), K9 and slip these 49 (52: 55: 58: 61: 66) sts onto a holder, P to end.
40 (43: 46: 49: 52: 57) sts.
Work each side of front separately.
Next row (RS): K3, M1 (for side seam inc), K to end.
Next row: Cast on and K 9 sts, P to end.
50 (53: 56: 59: 62: 67) sts.
Last 2 rows set the sts – front opening edge 9 sts in g st with all other sts in st st.
Working all side seam increases as set, inc 1 st at beg of 13th and 2 foll 14th rows.
53 (56: 59: 62: 65: 70) sts.
Work 5 rows, ending with a WS row.
Shape front slope
Next row (RS): K to last 14 sts, K2tog tbl (for front slope dec), K12.
Working all front slope decreases as set by last row, cont as follows:
Work 7 rows, dec 1 st at front slope edge of 4th of these rows and ending with a WS row.
51 (54: 57: 60: 63: 68) sts.
Shape armhole
Cast off 4 (4: 5: 5: 6: 6) sts at beg and dec 1 st at front slope edge of next row.
46 (49: 51: 54: 56: 61) sts.
Work 1 row.
Dec 1 st at armhole edge of next 3 (5: 5: 7: 7: 9) rows, then on foll 3 (3: 4: 4: 4: 6) alt rows, then on foll 4th row **and at same time** dec 1 st at front slope edge of 3rd and 2 (3: 3: 4: 4: 3) foll 4th rows, then on 0 (0: 0: 0: 0: 1) foll 6th row.
36 (36: 37: 37: 39: 40) sts.

Dec 1 st at front slope edge **only** on 2nd (4th: 2nd: 4th: 6th: 2nd) and 0 (1: 1: 1: 0: 0) foll 4th rows, then on 6 (5: 5: 5: 6: 6) foll 6th rows. 29 (29: 30: 30: 32: 33) sts.

Cont straight until left side of front matches back to start of shoulder shaping, ending with a WS row.

Shape shoulder

Cast off 7 (7: 7: 7: 8: 8) sts at beg of next and foll alt row, then 6 (6: 7: 7: 7: 8) sts at beg of foll alt row. 9 sts.

Inc 1 st at end of next row. 10 sts.

Cont in g st on these 10 sts only (for back neck border extension) until this strip measures 7 (7.5: 7.5: 8: 8: 8) cm, ending with a WS row. Break yarn and leave these sts on a holder.

Return to 49 (52: 55: 58: 61: 66) sts left on holder at base of front opening and rejoin yarn with RS facing.

Next row (RS): K to last 3 sts, M1 (for side seam inc), K3.

Next row: P to last 9 sts, K9.

50 (53: 56: 59: 62: 67) sts.

Last 2 rows set the sts – front opening edge 9 sts in g st with all other sts in st st.

Work 8 rows, ending with a WS row.

Next row (RS): K3, K2tog tbl, yfwd (to make a buttonhole), K to end.

Making a further 2 buttonholes in this way on every foll 16th row and noting that no further reference will be made to buttonholes, cont as follows:

Working all side seam increases as set, inc 1 st at end of 4th and 2 foll 14th rows.

53 (56: 59: 62: 65: 70) sts.

Work 5 rows, ending with a WS row.

Shape front slope

Next row (RS): K12, K2tog (for front slope dec), K to end.

Working all front slope decreases as set by last row, complete to match first side, reversing shapings.

SLEEVES (both alike)

Cast on 55 (57: 59: 61: 65: 67) sts using 2¾mm (US 2) needles.

Work in g st for 14 rows, ending with a WS row. Change to 3¼mm (US 3) needles.

Now working in st st throughout, beg with a K row, and all sleeve increases in same way as back and front side seam increases, cont as follows:

Inc 1 st at each end of 3rd and every foll 10th (10th: 10th: 10th: 12th: 12th) row to 69 (69: 67: 65: 83: 81) sts, then on every foll 12th (12th: 12th: 12th: -: 14th) row until there are 73 (75: 77: 79: -: 85) sts.

Cont straight until sleeve measures 33 (34: 35: 36: 37: 38) cm, ending with a WS row.

Shape top

Cast off 4 (4: 5: 5: 6: 6) sts at beg of next 2 rows.

65 (67: 67: 69: 71: 73) sts.

Dec 1 st at each end of next 5 rows, then on foll 2 alt rows, then on 2 foll 4th rows.

47 (49: 49: 51: 53: 55) sts.

work 1 row.

Dec 1 st at each end of next and every foll alt row until 37 sts rem, then on foll 5 rows, ending with a WS row.

Cast off rem 27 sts.

MAKING UP

Press all pieces with a warm iron over a damp cloth.

Join both shoulder seams using back stitch or mattress stitch if preferred. Graft the 2 sets of 9 back neck border extension sts together and then sew one edge to back neck edge. Join side seams, leaving side seams open below markers (for side seam slit openings). Join sleeve seams. Insert sleeves into armholes. Neatly sew cast-on sts at base of left front opening edge in place behind right front opening edge, then sew on buttons.

55 (56: 57: 58: 59: 60) cm
21½ (22: 22½: 22¾: 23¼: 23½) in

40.5 (43: 45.5: 48: 50.5: 54.5) cm
15 (17: 18: 19: 20: 21½) in

33 (34: 35: 36: 37: 38) cm
13 (13½: 13¾: 14: 14½: 15) in

Recommendation ○○

Please see pages 16 & 17 for photographs.

	XS	S	M	L	XL	XXL
To fit bust	**81**	**86**	**91**	**97**	**102**	**109 cm**
	32	34	36	38	40	43 in

Rowan Handknit Cotton

| | 12 | 13 | 14 | 14 | 15 | 16 | x 50gm |

Photographed in Black

Needles

1 pair 3mm (no 11) (US 2/3) needles
1 pair 3¾mm (no 9) (US 5) needles
Cable needle

Buttons - 5

Tension

25 sts and 30 rows to 10 cm measured over
pattern using 3¾mm (US 5) needles.

Special abbreviations

C4B = slip next 3 sts onto cable needle and
leave at back of work, K1, then K3 from cable
needle; **C4F** = slip next st onto cable needle
and leave at front of work, K3, then K1 from
cable needle; **Tw2L** = K into back of second st
on left needle, then K first st and slip both sts
off left needle together; **Tw2R** = K into front of
second st on left needle, then K first st and slip
both sts off left needle together.

Pattern note: When casting off across top
of cables it is advisable to work "K2tog" (or
"P2tog" on WS rows) at top of each cable to
avoid edge becoming too wide. All sts counts
given do NOT include these decreased sts but
relate to the original number of sts.

STUNNING
CLASSIC JACKET WITH UNDERSTATED CABLES

BACK

Cast on 93 (97: 103: 107: 113: 121) sts using
3mm (US 2/3) needles.
Work in g st for 10 rows, ending with a WS row.
Change to 3¾mm (US 5) needles.
Beg and ending rows as indicated and
following appropriate chart for size being
knitted, cont in patt from chart for body as
follows:
Work chart row 1.
108 (114: 120: 126: 132: 142) sts.
Now work chart rows 2 to 5, 6 times in total,
ending with a RS row.
Now repeating chart rows 6 to 9 **throughout**,
cont as follows:
Cont in patt until back measures 29 (29: 30:
30: 30: 30) cm, ending with
a WS row.

Shape armholes

Keeping patt correct, cast off 5 (5: 6: 6: 7: 7) sts
at beg of next 2 rows.
98 (104: 108: 114: 118: 128) sts.
Dec 1 st at each end of next 3 (5: 5: 7: 7: 9)
rows, then on foll 4 (4: 5: 4: 5: 6) alt rows.
84 (86: 88: 92: 94: 98) sts.
Cont straight until armhole measures 18 (19: 19:
20: 21: 22) cm, ending with a WS row.

Shape shoulders and back neck

Keeping patt correct, cast off 7 (7: 8: 8: 8: 9) sts
at beg of next 2 rows (see pattern note).
70 (72: 72: 76: 78: 80) sts.
Next row (RS): Cast off 7 (7: 8: 8: 8: 9) sts,
patt until there are 12 (12: 11: 12: 13: 13) sts
on right needle and turn, leaving rem sts on a
holder.
Work each side of neck separately.
Cast off 4 sts at beg of next row.
Cast off rem 8 (8: 7: 8: 9: 9) sts.
With RS facing, rejoin yarn and cast off centre
32 (34: 34: 36: 36: 36) sts, patt to end.
Complete to match first side, reversing
shapings.

POCKET LININGS (make 2)

Cast on 25 sts using 3¾mm (US 5) needles.
Beg with a P row, work in rev st st for 21 rows,
ending with a RS row.
Row 22 (WS): K5, M1, K7, M1, K1, M1, K8, M1,
K4. 29 sts.
Break yarn and leave sts on a holder.

LEFT FRONT

Cast on 53 (55: 58: 60: 63: 67) sts using 3mm
(US 2/3) needles.
Work in g st for 10 rows, ending with a WS row.
Change to 3¾mm (US 5) needles.
Beg and ending rows as indicated and
following appropriate chart for size being
knitted, cont in patt from chart for body as
follows:
Row 1 (RS): Work chart row 1 to last 5 sts, K5.
61 (64: 67: 70: 73: 78) sts.
This row sets the sts – front opening edge 5 sts
still in g st with all other sts in patt from chart.
Keeping sts correct as now set and now
working chart rows 2 to 5, 6 times in total, and
then repeating chart rows 6 to 9 **throughout**,
cont as follows:
Work 21 rows, ending with a WS row.

Place pocket

Next row (RS): Patt 11 (14: 17: 20: 23: 28) sts,
slip next 29 sts onto a holder and, in their
place, patt across 29 sts of first pocket lining,
patt rem 21 sts.
Cont straight until left front matches back to
beg of armhole shaping, ending with a WS row.

Shape armhole

Keeping patt correct, cast off 5 (5: 6: 6: 7: 7) sts
at beg of next row. 56 (59: 61: 64: 66: 71) sts.
Work 1 row.
Dec 1 st at armhole edge of next 3 (5: 5: 7: 7: 9)
rows, then on foll 4 (4: 5: 4: 5: 6) alt rows.
49 (50: 51: 53: 54: 56) sts.
Cont straight until 18 (18: 18: 20: 20: 20) rows
less have been worked than on back to start of
shoulder shaping, ending with a WS row.

Shape front neck

Next row (RS): Patt 30 (30: 31: 33: 34: 36) sts
and turn, leaving rem 19 (20: 20: 20: 20: 20) sts
on a holder (for neckband).
Keeping patt correct, dec 1 st at neck edge of
next 4 rows, then on foll 3 (3: 3: 4: 4: 4) alt
rows, then on foll 4th row.
22 (22: 23: 24: 25: 27) sts.
Work 3 rows, ending with
a WS row.

Shape shoulder

Keeping patt correct, cast off 7 (7: 8: 8: 8: 9) sts
at beg of next and foll alt row.
Work 1 row.
Cast off rem 8 (8: 7: 8: 9: 9) sts.

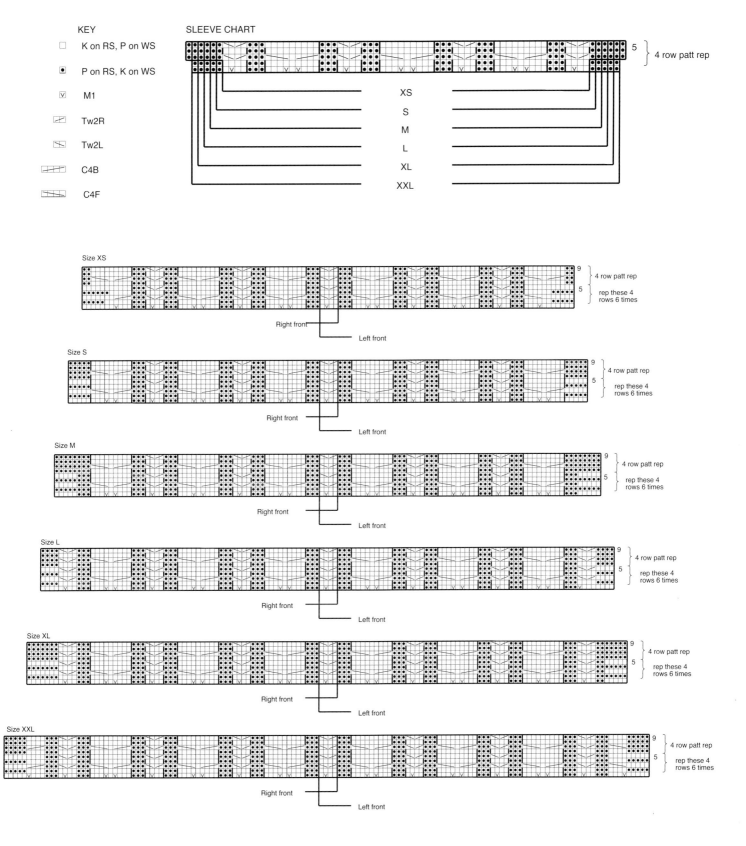

KEY

☐ K on RS, P on WS

● P on RS, K on WS

☑ M1

Tw2R

Tw2L

C4B

C4F

SLEEVE CHART

4 row patt rep

XS
S
M
L
XL
XXL

Size XS

9 } 4 row patt rep

5 } rep these 4 rows 6 times

Right front

Left front

Size S

9 } 4 row patt rep

5 } rep these 4 rows 6 times

Right front

Left front

Size M

9 } 4 row patt rep

5 } rep these 4 rows 6 times

Right front

Left front

Size L

9 } 4 row patt rep

5 } rep these 4 rows 6 times

Right front

Left front

Size XL

9 } 4 row patt rep

5 } rep these 4 rows 6 times

Right front

Left front

Size XXL

9 } 4 row patt rep

5 } rep these 4 rows 6 times

Right front

Left front

Mark positions for 5 buttons along left front opening edge – first button to come level with first RS row after placing pocket (this is 35th row from cast-on edge), last button to come 1 cm above start of neck shaping, and rem 3 buttons evenly spaced between.

RIGHT FRONT

Cast on 53 (55: 58: 60: 63: 67) sts using 3mm (US 2/3) needles.
Work in g st for 10 rows, ending with a WS row.
Change to 3¾mm (US 5) needles.
Beg and ending rows as indicated and following appropriate chart for size being knitted, cont in patt from chart for body as follows:
Row 1 (RS): K5, work chart row 1 to end.
61 (64: 67: 70: 73: 78) sts.
This row sets the sts – front opening edge 5 sts still in g st with all other sts in patt from chart.
Keeping sts correct as now set and now working chart rows 2 to 5, 6 times in total, and then repeating chart rows 6 to 9 **throughout**, cont as follows:
Work 21 rows, ending with a WS row.
Place pocket
Next row (RS): Patt 21 sts, slip next 29 sts onto a holder and, in their place, patt across 29 sts of second pocket lining, patt rem 11 (14: 17: 20: 23: 28) sts.
Work 1 row, ending with a WS row.
Next row (RS): K1, K2tog, yfwd (to make a buttonhole), patt to end.
Making a further 3 buttonholes in this way to correspond with positions marked for buttons on left front and noting that no further reference will be made to buttonholes, cont as follows:
Complete to match left front, reversing shapings and working first row of neck shaping as follows:
Shape front neck
Next row (RS): (K6, K2tog) twice, K1, K2tog, K0 (1: 1: 1: 1: 1) and slip these 16 (17: 17: 17: 17: 17) sts onto a holder (for neckband), patt to end.
30 (30: 31: 33: 34: 36) sts.

SLEEVES (both alike)

Cast on 51 (53: 55: 57: 59: 61) sts using 3mm (US 2/3) needles.
Work in g st for 10 rows, ending with a WS row.
Change to 3¾mm (US 5) needles.
Beg and ending rows as indicated, cont in patt from chart for sleeves as follows:
Work chart row 1.
61 (63: 65: 67: 69: 71) sts.

Now repeating chart rows 2 to 5 **throughout**, cont as follows:
Inc 1 st at each end of 2nd and every foll 12th (12th: 12th: 14th: 12th: 12th) row to 71 (69: 69: 79: 81: 79) sts, then on every foll 14th (14th: 14th: 16th: 14th: 14th) row until there are 75 (77: 79: 81: 85: 87) sts, taking inc sts into rev st st.
Cont straight until sleeve measures 33 (34: 35: 36: 37: 38) cm, ending with a WS row.
Shape top
Keeping patt correct, cast off 5 (5: 6: 6: 7: 7) sts at beg of next 2 rows.
65 (67: 67: 69: 71: 73) sts.
Dec 1 st at each end of next 3 rows, then on foll alt row, then on 3 foll 4th rows.
51 (53: 53: 55: 57: 59) sts.
Work 1 row.
Dec 1 st at each end of next and every foll alt row until 43 sts rem, then on foll 7 rows, ending with a WS row.
Cast off rem 29 sts.

MAKING UP

Press all pieces with a warm iron over a damp cloth.
Join both shoulder seams using back stitch or mattress stitch if preferred.
Neckband
With RS facing and using 3mm (US 2/3) needles, slip 16 (17: 17: 17: 17: 17) sts from right front holder onto right needle, rejoin yarn and pick up and knit 16 (16: 16: 18: 18: 18) sts up right side of front neck, 33 (35: 35: 37: 37: 37) sts from back, and 16 (16: 16: 18: 18: 18) sts down left side of front neck, then K across 19 (20: 20: 20: 20: 20) sts on left front holder as follows: K0 (1: 1: 1: 1: 1), K2tog, K1, (K2tog, K6) twice.
97 (101: 101: 107: 107: 107) sts.
Work in g st for 8 rows, making 5th buttonhole in 2nd of these rows and ending with a **RS** row.
Cast off knitwise (on **WS**).
Pocket tops (both alike)
Slip 29 sts on pocket holder onto 3mm (US 2/3) needles and rejoin yarn with RS facing.
Row 1 (RS): K4, K2tog, K6, K2tog, K1, K2tog, K6, K2tog, K4. 25 sts.
Work in g st for 8 rows, ending with a **RS** row.
Cast off knitwise (on **WS**).
Sew pocket linings in place on inside, then neatly sew down ends of pocket tops. Join side seams, leaving seams open for first 34 rows (for side seam openings). Join sleeve seams. Insert sleeves into armholes. Sew on buttons.

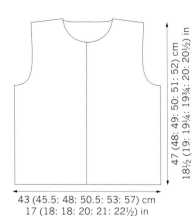

43 (45.5: 48: 50.5: 53: 57) cm
17 (18: 18: 20: 21: 22½) in

47 (48: 49: 50: 51: 52) cm
18½ (19: 19¼: 19¾: 20: 20½) in

33 (34: 35: 36: 37: 38) cm
13 (13½: 13¾: 14¼: 14½: 15) in

BEE

CHIC CROCHET BERET WITH SUBTLE STRIPES

Recommendation ◑◯
Please see pages 18 & 19 for photographs.

Rowan Summerlite DK
A   Black   2x 50gm
B   Silvery Blue   1x 50gm
C   Mocha   1x 50gm

One-colour version
Summerlite DK   2x 50gm

Crochet hooks
3.00mm (no 11) (US C2/D3) crochet hook
3.50mm (no 9) (US E4) crochet hook

Tension
First 4 rounds measure 8 cm in diameter using 3.50mm (US E4) crochet hook.

Crochet abbreviations
ch = chain; **dc** = double crochet; **dc2tog** = (insert hook into next st, yoh and draw loop through) twice, yoh and draw through all 3 loops on hook; **htr** = half treble; **sp** = space; **ss** = slip stitch; **tr** = treble.

One-colour version
Work as given for multi-colour version but using same colour throughout.

BERET

Make 5 ch using 3.50mm (US E4) crochet hook and yarn A and join with a ss to form a ring.
Round 1 (RS): 1 ch (does NOT count as st), 10 dc into ring, ss to first dc. 10 sts.
Round 2: 3 ch (counts as first tr), 1 tr into dc at base of 3 ch, 2 tr into each of next 9 dc, ss to top of 3 ch at beg of round. 20 sts.
Round 3: 3 ch (counts as first tr), 1 tr into st at base of 3 ch, 2 tr into each of next 19 sts, ss to top of 3 ch at beg of round. 40 sts.
Round 4: 3 ch (counts as first tr), 1 tr into st at base of 3 ch, 1 tr into each of next 3 sts, (2 tr into next st, 1 tr into each of next 3 sts) 9 times, ss to top of 3 ch at beg of round. 50 sts.
Round 5: 3 ch (counts as first tr), 1 tr into st at base of 3 ch, 1 tr into each of next 4 sts, (2 tr into next st, 1 tr into each of next 4 sts) 9 times, ss to top of 3 ch at beg of round. 60 sts.
Join in yarn B.
Round 6: Using yarn B, 2 ch (counts as first htr), 1 htr into st at base of 2 ch, 1 htr into each of next 5 sts, (2 htr into next st, 1 htr into each of next 5 sts) 9 times, ss to top of 2 ch at beg of round. 70 sts.
Round 7: Using yarn A, 3 ch (counts as first tr), 1 tr into st at base of 3 ch, 1 tr into each of next 6 sts, (2 tr into next st, 1 tr into each of next 6 sts) 9 times, ss to top of 3 ch at beg of round. 80 sts.
Round 8: Using yarn A, 4 ch (counts as first tr and 1 ch), 1 tr into st at base of 4 ch, 1 ch, miss 1 st, *(1 tr into next st, 1 ch, miss 1 st) 3 times**, (1 tr, 1 ch and 1 tr) into next st, 1 ch, miss 1 st, rep from * to end, ending last rep at **, ss to 3rd of 4 ch at beg of round. 100 sts.
Round 9: Using yarn A, 3 ch (counts as first tr), miss st at base of 3 ch, *1 tr into next ch sp**, 1 tr into next tr, rep from * to end, ending last rep at **, ss to top of 3 ch at beg of round.
Round 10: Using yarn B, 2 ch (counts as first htr), 1 htr into st at base of 2 ch, 1 htr into each of next 9 sts, (2 htr into next st, 1 htr into each of next 9 sts) 9 times, ss to top of 2 ch at beg of round. 110 sts.
Round 11: Using yarn A, 3 ch (counts as first tr), 1 tr into st at base of 3 ch, 1 tr into each of next 10 sts, (2 tr into next st, 1 tr into each of next 10 sts) 9 times, ss to top of 3 ch at beg of round. 120 sts.

Round 12: Using yarn A, 4 ch (counts as first tr and 1 ch), 1 tr into st at base of 4 ch, 1 ch, miss 1 st, *(1 tr into next st, 1 ch, miss 1 st) 5 times**, (1 tr, 1 ch and 1 tr) into next st, 1 ch, miss 1 st, rep from * to end, ending last rep at **, ss to 3rd of 4 ch at beg of round. 140 sts.
Round 13: As round 9.
Round 14: Using yarn B, 2 ch (counts as first htr), 1 htr into st at base of 2 ch, 1 htr into each of next 13 sts, (2 htr into next st, 1 htr into each of next 13 sts) 9 times, ss to top of 2 ch at beg of round. 150 sts.
Break off yarn B and cont using yarn A **only**.
Round 15: 3 ch (counts as first tr), 1 tr into st at base of 3 ch, 1 tr into each of next 14 sts, (2 tr into next st, 1 tr into each of next 14 sts) 9 times, ss to top of 3 ch at beg of round. 160 sts.
Round 16: 4 ch (counts as first tr and 1 ch), miss st at base of 4 ch and next st, *1 tr into next st, 1 ch, miss 1 st, rep from * to end, ss to 3rd of 4 ch at beg of round.
Round 17: As round 9.
Round 18: As round 16.
Round 19: As round 9.
Round 20: As round 16.
Round 21: Ss into first ch sp, 3 ch (counts as first tr), *(1 tr into next tr, 1 tr into next ch sp) 3 times**, miss 1 tr, 1 tr into next ch sp, rep from * to end, ending last rep at **, ss to top of 3 ch at beg of round. 140 sts.
Round 22: As round 16.
Round 23: 3 ch (does NOT count as st), miss st at base of 3 ch, 1 tr into next st, (miss 1 st, 1 tr into each of next 2 sts) 46 times, ss to top of first tr (remembering that 3 ch at beg of round does NOT count as a st). 93 sts.
Change to 3.00mm (US C2/D3) crochet hook.
Round 24: 1 ch (does NOT count as st), (1 dc into each of next 7 sts, dc2tog over next 2 sts) 10 times, 1 dc into each of last 3 sts, ss to first dc. 83 sts.
Round 25: 1 ch (does NOT count as st), 1 dc into each st to end, ss to first dc.
Round 26: As round 25.
Join in yarn C.
Round 27: Using yarn C, 2 ch (counts as first htr), miss st at base of 2 ch, 1 htr into each dc to end, ss to top of 2 ch at beg of round.
Break off yarn C and cont using yarn A **only**.
Rounds 28 and 28: As round 25. Fasten off.

Recommendation ○○
Please see pages 22 & 23 for photographs.

	XS	S	M	L	XL	XXL	
To fit bust	**81**	**86**	**91**	**97**	**102**	**109 cm**
	32	34	36	38	40	43	in

Rowan Cotton Glacé

	6	7	7	8	8	9	50gm

Photographed in Dawn Grey

Needles
1 pair 2¾mm (no 12) (US 2) needles
1 pair 3¼mm (no 10) (US 3) needles
Cable needle

Tension
24 sts and 34 rows to 10 cm measured over trellis pattern, 23 sts and 32 rows to 10 cm measured over double moss stitch, both using 3¼mm (US 3) needles.

Special abbreviations
Tw2L = K into back of second st on left needle, then K first st and slip both sts off left needle together; **Tw2R** = K into front of second st on left needle, then K first st and slip both sts off left needle together.

GASP
NEAT SWEATER IN LATTICE AND CABLES

BACK and FRONT (both alike)
Cast on 108 (115: 123: 129: 138: 148) sts using 2¾mm (US 2) needles.
Row 1 (RS): K0 (0: 0: 1: 0: 0), P0 (1: 0: 2: 0: 0), *K3, P2, rep from * to last 3 (4: 3: 1: 3: 3) sts, K3 (3: 3: 1: 3: 3), P0 (1: 0: 0: 0: 0).
Row 2: P0 (0: 0: 1: 0: 0), K0 (1: 0: 2: 0: 0), *P3, K2, rep from * to last 3 (4: 3: 1: 3: 3) sts, P3 (3: 3: 1: 3: 3), K0 (1: 0: 0: 0: 0).
These 2 rows form rib.
Cont in rib for a further 31 rows, ending with a **RS** row.
Row 34 (WS): P0 (0: 0: 1: 0: 0), K0 (1: 0: 2: 0: 0), (P1, P2tog, K2) 3 (3: 4: 4: 5: 6) times, P1, P2tog, K1, M1, K1, P1, P2tog, (K2, P1, P2tog) 13 (14: 14: 14: 15: 15) times, K1, M1, K1, P1, P2tog, (K2, P1, P2tog) 3 (3: 4: 4: 5: 6) times, K0 (1: 0: 2: 0: 0), P0 (0: 0: 1: 0: 0).
88 (94: 100: 106: 112: 120) sts.
Change to 3¼mm (US 3) needles.
Now work in patt as follows:
Row 1 (RS): K0 (1: 0: 1: 0: 0), (P1, K1) 3 (3: 5: 6: 7: 9) times, P2, Tw2R, P2, Tw2L, P2, (P1, Tw2R, P1) 14 (15: 15: 15: 16: 16) times, P2, Tw2R, P2, Tw2L, P2, (K1, P1) 3 (3: 5: 6: 7: 9) times, K0 (1: 0: 1: 0: 0).
Row 2: K0 (1: 0: 1: 0: 0), (P1, K1) 3 (3: 5: 6: 7: 9) times, (K2, P2) twice, K2, (K1, P2, K1) 14 (15: 15: 15: 16: 16) times, (K2, P2) twice, K2, (K1, P1) 3 (3: 5: 6: 7: 9) times, K0 (1: 0: 1: 0: 0).
Row 3: Inc in first st, P1 (0: 1: 0: 1: 1), (K1, P1) 2 (3: 4: 6: 6: 8) times, P2, Tw2R, P2, Tw2L, P2, *K2tog, (yfwd) twice, sl 1, K1, psso, rep from * 13 (14: 14: 14: 15: 15) times more, P2, Tw2R, P2, Tw2L, P2, (P1, K1) 2 (3: 4: 6: 6: 8) times, P1 (0: 1: 0: 1: 1), inc in last st.
90 (96: 102: 108: 114: 122) sts.
Row 4: P1 (0: 1: 0: 1: 1), (K1, P1) 3 (4: 5: 7: 7: 9) times, (K2, P2) twice, K2, *P1, (K1, P1) into double yfwd of previous row, P1, rep from * 13 (14: 14: 14: 15: 15) times more, (K2, P2) twice, K2, (P1, K1) 3 (4: 5: 7: 7: 9) times, P1 (0: 1: 0: 1: 1).
Row 5: K1 (0: 1: 0: 1: 1), (P1, K1) 3 (4: 5: 7: 7: 9) times, P2, Tw2R, P2, Tw2L, P2, K1, P1, (P1, Tw2L, P1) 13 (14: 14: 14: 15: 15) times, P1, K1, P2, Tw2R, P2, Tw2L, P2, (K1, P1) 3 (4: 5: 7: 7: 9) times, K1 (0: 1: 0: 1: 1).

Row 6: K1 (0: 1: 0: 1: 1), (P1, K1) 3 (4: 5: 7: 7: 9) times, (K2, P2) twice, K2, P1, K1, (K1, P2, K1) 13 (14: 14: 14: 15: 15) times, K1, P1, (K2, P2) twice, K2, (K1, P1) 3 (4: 5: 7: 7: 9) times, K1 (0: 1: 0: 1: 1).
Row 7: P1 (0: 1: 0: 1: 1), (K1, P1) 3 (4: 5: 7: 7: 9) times, P2, Tw2R, P2, Tw2L, P2, yon, sl 1, K1, psso, *K2tog, (yfwd) twice, sl 1, K1, psso, rep from * 12 (13: 13: 13: 14: 14) times more, K2tog, yfrn, P2, Tw2R, P2, Tw2L, P2, (P1, K1) 3 (4: 5: 7: 7: 9) times, P1 (0: 1: 0: 1: 1).
Row 8: P1 (0: 1: 0: 1: 1), (K1, P1) 3 (4: 5: 7: 7: 9) times, (K2, P2) twice, K3, P1, *P1, (K1, P1) into double yfwd of previous row, P1, rep from * 12 (13: 13: 13: 14: 14) times more, P1, K1, (K2, P2) twice, K2, (K1, P1) 3 (4: 5: 7: 7: 9) times, P1 (0: 1: 0: 1: 1).
These 8 rows form patt and start side seam shaping.
Keeping sts correct as now set, cont as follows:
Inc 1 st at each end of 5th and 3 foll 10th rows, taking inc sts into double moss st.
98 (104: 110: 116: 122: 130) sts.
Cont straight until work measures 28 (28: 29: 29: 29: 29) cm, ending with a WS row.
Shape armholes
Keeping patt correct, cast off 5 (5: 6: 6: 7: 7) sts at beg of next 2 rows.
88 (94: 98: 104: 108: 116) sts.
Dec 1 st at each end of next 1 (3: 3: 5: 5: 7) rows, then on foll 2 (2: 3: 3: 4: 4) alt rows, then on foll 4th row.
80 (82: 84: 86: 88: 92) sts.
Cont straight until armhole measures 13 (14: 14: 15: 16: 17) cm, ending with a WS row.
Shape neck
Next row (RS): Patt 16 (16: 17: 17: 18: 20) sts and turn, leaving rem sts on a holder.
Work each side of neck separately.
Keeping patt correct, dec 1 st at neck edge of next 4 rows, then on foll 2 alt rows, then on foll 4th row.
9 (9: 10: 10: 11: 13) sts.
Work 3 rows, ending with a WS row.
Shape shoulder
Cast off rem 9 (9: 10: 10: 11: 13) sts.
With RS facing, rejoin yarn and cast off centre 48 (50: 50: 52: 52: 52) sts, patt to end.
Complete to match first side, reversing shapings.

SLEEVES (both alike)

Cast on 80 (82: 84: 88: 90: 92) sts using 2¾mm (US 2) needles.

Row 1 (RS): K0 (0: 1: 0: 0: 0), P1 (2: 2: 0: 1: 2), *K3, P2, rep from * to last 4 (0: 1: 3: 4: 0) sts, K3 (0: 1: 3: 3: 0), P1 (0: 0: 0: 1: 0).

Row 2: P0 (0: 1: 0: 0: 0), K1 (2: 2: 0: 1: 2), *P3, K2, rep from * to last 4 (0: 1: 3: 4: 0) sts, P3 (0: 1: 3: 3: 0), K1 (0: 0: 0: 1: 0).

These 2 rows form rib.

Cont in rib for a further 17 rows, ending with a **RS** row.

Row 20 (WS): P0 (0: 1: 0: 0: 0), K1 (2: 2: 0: 1: 2), (P1, P2tog, K2) 3 (3: 3: 4: 4: 4) times, P1, P2tog, K1, M1, K1, P1, P2tog, (K2, P1, P2tog) 7 times, K1, M1, K1, P1, P2tog, (K2, P1, P2tog) 3 (3: 3: 4: 4: 4) times, K1 (2: 2: 0: 1: 2), P0 (0: 1: 0: 0: 0). 66 (68: 70: 72: 74: 76) sts.

Change to 3¼mm (US 3) needles.

Now work in patt as follows:

Row 1 (RS): K1 (0: 1: 0: 1: 0), (P1, K1) 3 (4: 4: 5: 5: 6) times, P2, Tw2R, P2, Tw2L, P2, (P1, Tw2R, P1) 8 times, P2, Tw2R, P2, Tw2L, P2, (K1, P1) 3 (4: 4: 5: 5: 6) times, K1 (0: 1: 0: 1: 0).

Row 2: K1 (0: 1: 0: 1: 0), (P1, K1) 3 (4: 4: 5: 5: 6) times, (K2, P2) twice, K2, (K1, P2, K1) 8 times, (K2, P2) twice, K2, (K1, P1) 3 (4: 4: 5: 5: 6) times, K1 (0: 1: 0: 1: 0).

These 2 rows **set position** of patt as given for back and front.

Keeping patt correct as now set, cont in patt, shaping sides by inc 1 st at each end of next and 1 (1: 1: 1: 2: 2) foll 10th (10th: 10th: 10th: 6th: 6th) rows, taking inc sts into double moss st. 70 (72: 74: 76: 80: 82) sts.

Cont straight until sleeve measures 12 (13: 13: 14: 15: 15) cm, ending with a WS row.

Shape top

Keeping patt correct, cast off 5 (5: 6: 6: 7: 7) sts at beg of next 2 rows.

60 (62: 62: 64: 66: 68) sts.

Dec 1 st at each end of next and foll 2 alt rows, then on 4 foll 4th rows.

46 (48: 48: 50: 52: 54) sts.

Work 1 row.

Dec 1 st at each end of next and every foll alt row until 34 sts rem, then on foll 3 rows, ending with a WS row.

Cast off rem 28 sts.

MAKING UP

Press all pieces with a warm iron over a damp cloth.

Join right shoulder seam using back stitch or mattress stitch if preferred.

Neckband

With RS facing and using 2¾mm (US 2) needles, pick up and knit 13 sts down left side of front neck, 48 (50: 50: 52: 52: 52) sts from front, 12 sts up right side of front neck, 12 sts down right side of back neck, 48 (50: 50: 52: 52: 52) sts from back, and 13 sts up left side of back neck.

146 (150: 150: 154: 154: 154) sts.

Starting with a K row, work in rev st st for 5 rows, ending with a WS row.

Cast off **purlwise** (on RS).

Join left shoulder and neckband seam. Join side seams. Join sleeve seams. Insert sleeves into armholes.

40.5 (43: 45.5: 48: 50.5: 54.5) cm
16 (17: 18: 19: 20: 21½) in

46 (47: 48: 49: 50: 51) cm
18 (18½: 19: 19¼: 19¾: 20) in

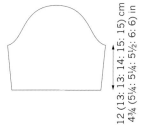

12 (13: 13: 14: 15: 15) cm
4¾ (5¼: 5¼: 5½: 6: 6) in

STARTLE

Recommendation ○
Please see pages 24 & 25 for photographs.

	XS	S	M	L	XL	XXL	
To fit bust	**81**	**86**	**91**	**97**	**102**	**109**	**cm**
	32	34	36	38	40	43	in

Rowan Handknit Cotton and Summerlite 4 ply
Handknit Cotton

	9	10	10	11	11	12	x 50gm

Summerlite 4 ply

	4	5	5	6	6	6	x 50gm

Photographed in Handknit Cotton in Black and
Summerlite 4 ply in Washed Linen

Needles
1 pair 6½mm (no 3) (US 10½) needles

Tension
14 sts and 18 rows to 10 cm measured over
stocking stitch using 6½mm (US 10½) needles
and one strand each of Handknit Cotton and
Summerlite 4 ply held together.

Special note: We found it preferable to knit the
two yarns together from separate balls rather
than winding them together.

BACK
Cast on 65 (69: 73: 77: 81: 85) sts using
6½mm (US 10½) needles and one strand each
of Handknit Cotton and Summerlite 4 ply held
together.
Beg with a K row, work in st st until back
measures 39 (39: 40: 40: 40: 40) cm, ending
with a WS row.
Shape armholes
Cast off 3 (3: 4: 4: 5: 5) sts at beg of next
2 rows. 59 (63: 65: 69: 71: 75) sts.
Next row (RS): K3, K2tog, K to last 5 sts,
K2tog tbl, K3.
Next row: P3, P2tog tbl, P to last 5 sts,
P2tog, P3.
Working all armhole decreases as set by last
2 rows, dec 1 st at each end of next 1 (1: 1:
3: 3: 3) rows, then on foll 1 (2: 2: 2: 2: 3) alt
rows, then on foll 4th row.
49 (51: 53: 53: 55: 57) sts.
Cont straight until armhole measures 18 (19:
19: 20: 21: 22) cm, ending with a WS row.
Shape shoulders and back neck
Cast off 5 (5: 5: 5: 5: 6) sts at beg of next 2
rows. 39 (41: 43: 43: 45: 45) sts.
Next row (RS): Cast off 5 (5: 5: 5: 5: 6) sts, K
until there are 9 (9: 10: 9: 10: 9) sts on right
needle and turn, leaving rem sts on a holder.
Work each side of neck separately.
Cast off 4 sts at beg of next row.
Cast off rem 5 (5: 6: 5: 6: 5) sts.
With RS facing, rejoin yarns and cast off centre
11 (13: 13: 15: 15: 15) sts, K to end.
Complete to match first side, reversing
shapings.

POCKET LININGS (make 2)
Cast on 16 (16: 16: 18: 18: 18) sts using
6½mm (US 10½) needles and one strand each
of Handknit Cotton and Summerlite 4 ply held
together.
Beg with a K row, work in st st for 21 (21: 21:
23: 23: 23) rows, ending with a **RS** row.
Break yarn and leave sts on a holder.

LEFT FRONT
Cast on 37 (39: 41: 43: 45: 47) sts using
6½mm (US 10½) needles and one strand
each of Handknit Cotton and Summerlite
4 ply held together.

Row 1 (RS): K to last st, pick up loop lying
between needles and place this loop on right
needle (**Note**: This loop does **NOT** count as a st),
with yarn still at back (WS) of work slip last st
purlwise.
Row 2: P tog the first st and the picked-up
loop, P to end.
Last 2 rows set the sts – slip st edging at front
opening edge of rows and all other sts in st st.
Keeping sts correct as now set throughout,
cont as follows:
Work 22 (22: 22: 22: 24: 24) rows, ending with
a WS row.
Place pocket
Next row (RS): K7 (8: 9: 9: 10: 11),
cast off next 16 (16: 16: 18: 18: 18) sts,
patt to end.
Next row: Patt 14 (15: 16: 16: 17: 18) sts,
P across 16 (16: 16: 18: 18: 18) sts of first
pocket lining, P7 (8: 9: 9: 10: 11).
Cont straight until 16 rows less have been
worked than on back to start of armhole
shaping, ending with a WS row.
Shape front slope
Next row (RS): K to last 7 sts, K2tog tbl, patt
5 sts.
Working all front slope shaping as set by last
row, cont as follows:
Dec 1 st at front slope edge of 4th and 2 foll
4th rows. 33 (35: 37: 39: 41: 43) sts.
Work 3 rows, ending with a WS row.
Shape armhole
Cast off 3 (3: 4: 4: 5: 5) sts at beg and dec
0 (1: 1: 1: 1: 1) st at end of next row.
30 (31: 32: 34: 35: 37) sts.
Work 1 row.
Working all armhole decreases as set by back,
dec 1 st at armhole edge of next 3 (3: 3: 5:
5: 5) rows, then on foll 1 (2: 2: 2: 2: 3) alt
rows, then on foll 4th row **and at same time**
dec 1 st at front slope edge of next (3rd: 3rd:
3rd: 3rd: 3rd) and 0 (0: 0: 2: 1: 0) foll 4th
rows, then on 1 (1: 1: 0: 1: 2) foll 6th rows.
23 (23: 24: 23: 24: 25) sts.
Dec 1 st at front slope edge **only** on 4th (4th:
4th: 4th: 6th: 6th) and 2 foll 6th rows.
20 (20: 21: 20: 21: 22) sts.
Cont straight until left front matches back to
start of shoulder shaping, ending with
a WS row.

Shape shoulder

Cast off 5 (5: 5: 5: 5: 6) sts at beg of next and foll alt row, then 5 (5: 6: 5: 6: 5) sts at beg of foll alt row. 5 sts.

Inc 1 st at end of next row.

Cont as set on these 6 sts **only** (for back neck border extension) until this strip measures 6.5 (7: 7: 7.5: 7.5: 7.5) cm, ending with a WS row. Break yarn and leave these 6 sts on a holder.

RIGHT FRONT

Cast on 37 (39: 41: 43: 45: 47) sts using 6½mm (US 10½) needles and one strand each of Handknit Cotton and Summerlite 4 ply held together.

Row 1 (RS): Knit.

Row 2: P to last st, pick up loop lying between needles and place this loop on right needle (**Note**: This loop does **NOT** count as a st), slip last st **knitwise**.

Row 3: K tog **tbl** the first st and the picked-up loop, K to end.

Last 2 rows set the sts – slip st edging at front opening edge of rows and all other sts in st st. Keeping sts correct as now set throughout, cont as follows:

Work 19 (19: 19: 21: 21: 21) rows, ending with a WS row.

Place pocket

Next row (RS): Patt 14 (15: 16: 16: 17: 18) sts, cast off next 16 (16: 16: 18: 18: 18) sts, K to end.

Next row: P7 (8: 9: 9: 10: 11), P across 16 (16: 16: 18: 18: 18) sts of second pocket lining, patt 14 (15: 16: 16: 17: 18) sts.

Cont straight until 16 rows less have been worked than on back to start of armhole shaping, ending with a WS row.

Shape front slope

Next row (RS): Patt 5 sts, K2tog, K to end.

Working all front slope shaping as set by last row, complete to match left front, reversing shapings.

SLEEVES (both alike)

Cast on 30 (32: 34: 34: 36: 38) sts using 6½mm (US 10½) needles and one strand each of Handknit Cotton and Summerlite 4 ply held together.

Starting with a K row, work in st st throughout as follows:

Work 16 rows, ending with a WS row.

Next row (RS): K3, M1, K to last 3 sts, M1, K3.

Working all sleeve increases as set by last row, inc 1 st at each end of 8th (10th: 10th: 8th: 8th: 8th) and 0 (0: 0: 2: 1: 1) foll 8th rows, then on 5 (5: 4: 4: 5: 5) foll 10th rows, then on 0 (0: 1: 0: 0: 0) foll 12th rows.

44 (46: 48: 50: 52: 54) sts.

Cont straight until sleeve measures 46 (47: 48: 49: 50: 51) cm, ending with a WS row.

Shape top

Cast off 3 (3: 4: 4: 5: 5) sts at beg of next 2 rows. 38 (40: 40: 42: 42: 44) sts.

Dec 1 st at each end of next and foll alt row, then on 2 foll 4th rows.

30 (32: 32: 34: 34: 36) sts.

Work 1 row.

Dec 1 st at each end of next and every foll alt row until 26 sts rem, then on foll 3 rows, ending with a WS row.

Cast off rem 20 sts.

MAKING UP

Press all pieces with a warm iron over a damp cloth. Join both shoulder seams using back stitch or mattress stitch if preferred. Graft together both sets of 6 back neck border extension sts left on holders, then sew one edge to back neck. Join side seams. Join sleeve seams. Insert sleeves into armholes. Sew pocket linings in place on inside.

57 (58: 59: 60: 61: 62) cm
22½ (22¾: 23¼: 23¼: 23¾: 24: 24¾) in

45.5 (48: 50.5: 53: 55.5: 59.5) cm
18 (19: 20: 21: 22: 23½) in

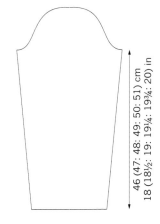

46 (47: 48: 49: 50: 51) cm
18 (18½: 19: 19¼: 19¾: 20) in

WISTFUL
NEAT CARDIGAN WITH CROCHET TRIMS

Recommendation ◯◯
Please see pages 28 & 29 for photographs.

	XS	S	M	L	XL	XXL	
To fit bust	**81**	**86**	**91**	**97**	**102**	**109**	cm
	32	34	36	38	40	43	in

Rowan Summerlite 4 ply

	7	8	8	9	9	10	x 50gm

Photographed in Washed Linen

Needles
1 pair 4½mm (no 7) (US 7) needles
3.50mm (no 9) (US E4) crochet hook

Tension
19 sts and 25 rows to 10 cm measured over
stocking stitch using 4½mm (US 7) needles
and yarn DOUBLE.

Crochet abbreviations
dc = double crochet; **ss** = slip stitch.

Special note: We found it preferable to knit the
two yarns together from separate balls rather
than winding them together.

BACK
Cast on 82 (86: 90: 96: 100: 108) sts using
4½mm (US 7) needles and yarn DOUBLE.
Beg with a K row, work in st st throughout
as follows:
Cont straight until back measures 33 (33: 34:
34: 34: 34) cm, ending with a WS row.
Shape raglan armholes
Cast off 4 sts at beg of next 2 rows.
74 (78: 82: 88: 92: 100) sts.
Work 2 (2: 0: 0: 0: 0) rows, ending with a WS row.
Next row (RS): K1, K2tog, K to last 3 sts,
K2tog tbl, K1.
Next row: (P1, P2tog tbl) 0 (0: 0: 1: 1: 1)
times, P to last 0 (0: 0: 3: 3: 3) sts, (P2tog, P1)
0 (0: 0: 1: 1: 1) times. 72 (76: 80: 84: 88: 96) sts.
Working all raglan armhole decreases as set by
last 2 rows, dec 1 st at each end of 3rd (3rd:
next: next: next: next) and foll 0 (0: 0: 0: 0: 6)
rows, then on foll 20 (21: 23: 24: 26: 24) alt
rows. 30 (32: 32: 34: 34: 34) sts.
Work 1 row, ending with a WS row.
Cast off.

POCKET LININGS (make 2)
Cast on 22 (22: 22: 24: 24: 24) sts using
4½mm (US 7) needles and yarn DOUBLE.
Beg with a K row, work in st st for 19 (19: 19:
21: 21: 21) rows, ending with a **RS** row.
Break yarn and leave sts on a holder.

LEFT FRONT
Cast on 43 (45: 47: 50: 52: 56) sts using
4½mm (US 7) needles and yarn DOUBLE.
Beg with a K row, work in st st throughout as
follows:
Work 28 (28: 28: 30: 30: 30) rows, ending with
a WS row.
Place pocket
Next row (RS): K7 (8: 9: 9: 10: 12), cast off
next 22 (22: 22: 24: 24: 24) sts, K to end.
Next row: P14 (15: 16: 17: 18: 20), P across
22 (22: 22: 24: 24: 24) sts of first pocket
lining, P7 (8: 9: 9: 10: 12).
Cont straight until left front matches back to
beg of raglan armhole shaping, ending
with a WS row.
Shape raglan armhole
Cast off 4 sts at beg of next row.
39 (41: 43: 46: 48: 52) sts.

Work 3 (3: 1: 1: 1: 1) rows, ending with a WS row.
Working all raglan armhole decreases as set by
back, dec 1 st at raglan armhole edge of next
and foll 0 (0: 0: 2: 2: 8) rows, then on 1 (1: 0:
0: 0: 0) foll 4th row, then on foll 14 (15: 18:
17: 19: 17) alt rows.
23 (24: 24: 26: 26: 26) sts.
Work 1 row, ending with a WS row.
Shape front neck
Next row (RS): K1, K2tog, K8 (8: 8: 10: 10: 10),
cast off rem 12 (13: 13: 13: 13: 13) sts.
Break yarn.
Rejoin yarn to rem 10 (10: 10: 12: 12: 12) sts
with **WS** facing and cont as follows:
Dec 1 st at neck edge of next 4 rows, then on
foll 0 [0: 0: 1: 1: 1) alt row **and at same time**
dec 1 st at raglan armhole edge of 2nd and foll
1 (1: 1: 2: 2: 2) alt rows. 4 sts.
Work 1 row, ending with a WS row.
Next row (RS): K1, K3tog.
Next row: P2.
Next row: K2tog and fasten off.

RIGHT FRONT
Cast on 43 (45: 47: 50: 52: 56) sts using
4½mm (US 7) needles and yarn DOUBLE.
Beg with a K row, work in st st throughout as
follows:
Work 28 (28: 28: 30: 30: 30) rows, ending with
a WS row.
Place pocket
Next row (RS): K14 (15: 16: 17: 18: 20), cast
off next 22 (22: 22: 24: 24: 24) sts, K to end.
Next row: P7 (8: 9: 9: 10: 12), P across
22 (22: 22: 24: 24: 24) sts of second pocket
lining, P14 (15: 16: 17: 18: 20).
Complete to match left front, reversing
shapings and working first row of neck shaping
as follows:
Shape front neck
Next row (RS): Cast off 12 (13: 13: 13: 13: 13) sts,
K to last 3 sts, K2tog tbl, K1.
10 (10: 10: 12: 12: 12) sts.

SLEEVES (both alike)
Cast on 53 (55: 55: 57: 61: 63) sts using
4½mm (US 7) needles and yarn DOUBLE.
Beg with a K row, work in st st throughout as
follows:
Work 14 rows, ending with a WS row.

Next row (RS): K3, M1, K to last 3 sts, M1, K3.
55 (57: 57: 59: 63: 65) sts.
Cont straight until sleeve measures 10 (10: 11:
11: 12: 12) cm, ending with a WS row.

Shape raglan
Cast off 4 sts at beg of next 2 rows.
47 (49: 49: 51: 55: 57) sts.
Working all raglan decreases in same way as
raglan armhole decreases, dec 1 st at each end
of 3rd and 7 foll 4th rows, then on every foll alt
row until 19 sts rem.
Work 1 row, ending with a WS row.

Left sleeve only
Dec 1 st at each end of next row, then cast off
4 sts at beg of foll row. 13 sts.
Dec 1 st at beg of next row, then cast off 6 sts
at beg of foll row.

Right sleeve only
Cast off 5 sts at beg and dec 1 st at end of next
row. 13 sts.
Work 1 row.
Cast off 6 sts at beg and dec 1 st at end of next
row.
Work 1 row.

Both sleeves
Cast off rem 6 sts.

MAKING UP
Press all pieces with a warm iron over a damp cloth.
Join all raglan seams using back stitch or
mattress stitch if preferred. Join side and
sleeve seams, leaving side seams open for first
26 rows (for side seam slit openings). Neatly
sew pocket linings in place on inside.

Edging
With RS facing, using 3.50mm (US E4) crochet
hook and yarn SINGLE, attach yarn to lower
edge of back and work one round of dc around
entire outer edge of cardigan, working 2 dc into
corner points and ending with ss to first dc, do
NOT turn.
Now work one round of crab st (dc worked
from left to right, instead of right to left) around
entire outer edge, ending with ss to first st.
Fasten off.
In same way, work edging around cast-on
edges of sleeves, and across pocket opening
edges.

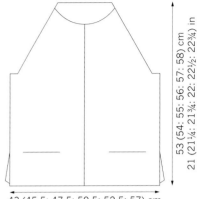

53 (54: 55: 56: 57: 58) cm
21 (21¼: 21¼: 22: 22½: 22¾) in

43 (45.5: 47.5: 50.5: 52.5: 57) cm
17 (18: 18¾: 19¾: 20¾: 22½) in

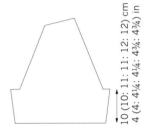

10 (10: 11: 11: 12: 12) cm
4 (4: 4¼: 4¼: 4¾: 4¾) in

Recommendation ○○

Please see pages 26 & 27 for photographs.

	XS	S	M	L	XL	XXL	
To fit bust	**81**	**86**	**91**	**97**	**102**	**109 cm**	
	32	34	36	38	40	43	in

Rowan Creative Linen

	5	6	6	6	7	7	x 100gm

Photographed in Stormy

Needles

1 pair 3¾mm (no 9) (US 5) needles
1 pair 4½mm (no 7) (US 7) needles
Cable needle

Tension

22 sts and 28 rows to 10 cm measured over trellis pattern, 20½ sts and 28 rows to 10 cm measured over double moss stitch, both using 4½mm (US 7) needles.

Special abbreviations

C4B = slip next 3 sts onto cable needle and leave at back of work, K1, then K3 from cable needle; **C4F** = slip next st onto cable needle and leave at front of work, K3, then K1 from cable needle; **Tw2L** = K into back of second st on left needle, then K first st and slip both sts off left needle together; **Tw2R** = K into front of second st on left needle, then K first st and slip both sts off left needle together.

AMARA
SWEATER WORKED IN LATTICE & CABLES

BACK

Cast on 102 (108: 114: 118: 124: 132) sts using 3¾mm (US 5) needles.
Row 1 (RS): P2 (1: 0: 2: 1: 1), K2, *P2, K2, rep from * to last 2 (1: 0: 2: 1: 1) sts, P2 (1: 0: 2: 1: 1).
Row 2: K2 (1: 0: 2: 1: 1), P2, *K2, P2, rep from * to last 2 (1: 0: 2: 1: 1) sts, K2 (1: 0: 2: 1: 1).
These 2 rows form rib.
Cont in rib for a further 21 rows, ending with a **RS** row.
Row 24 (WS): Rib 4 (7: 10: 12: 15: 19), K2tog, P2, K2tog, rib 16, P2tog, rib 8, M1, rib 28, M1, rib 10, P2tog, rib 16, K2tog, P2, K2tog, rib 4 (7: 10: 12: 15: 19).
98 (104: 110: 114: 120: 128) sts.
Change to 4½mm (US 7) needles.
Now work in patt as follows:
Row 1 (RS): P0 (1: 0: 0: 1: 1), (K1, P1) 5 (6: 8: 9: 10: 12) times, (P2, Tw2R) twice, P2, C4B, K1, C4F, P2, Tw2L, P3, (Tw2R, P2) 7 times, P1, Tw2R, P2, C4B, K1, C4F, P2, (Tw2L, P2) twice, (P1, K1) 5 (6: 8: 9: 10: 12) times, P0 (1: 0: 0: 1: 1).
Row 2: P0 (1: 0: 0: 1: 1), (K1, P1) 5 (6: 8: 9: 10: 12) times, (K2, P2) twice, K2, P9, K2, P2, K3, (P2, K2) 6 times, P2, K3, P2, K2, P9, K2, (P2, K2) twice, (P1, K1) 5 (6: 8: 9: 10: 12) times, P0 (1: 0: 0: 1: 1).
Row 3: K0 (1: 0: 0: 1: 1), (P1, K1) 5 (6: 8: 9: 10: 12) times, (P2, Tw2R) twice, P2, K9, P2, Tw2L, P2, *K2tog, (yfwd) twice, sl 1, K1, psso, rep from * 6 times more, P2, Tw2R, P2, K9, P2, (Tw2L, P2) twice, (K1, P1) 5 (6: 8: 9: 10: 12) times, K0 (1: 0: 0: 1: 1).
Row 4: K0 (1: 0: 0: 1: 1), (P1, K1) 5 (6: 8: 9: 10: 12) times, (K2, P2) twice, K2, P9, K2, P2, K2, *P1, (K1, P1) into double yfwd of previous row, P1, rep from * 6 times more, K2, P2, K2, P9, K2, (P2, K2) twice, (K1, P1) 5 (6: 8: 9: 10: 12) times, K0 (1: 0: 0: 1: 1).
Row 5: P0 (1: 0: 0: 1: 1), (K1, P1) 5 (6: 8: 9: 10: 12) times, (P2, Tw2R) twice, P2, C4B, K1, C4F, P2, Tw2L, P2, K1, (P2, Tw2L) 6 times, P2, K1, P2, Tw2R, P2, C4B, K1, C4F, P2, (Tw2L, P2) twice, (P1, K1) 5 (6: 8: 9: 10: 12) times, P0 (1: 0: 0: 1: 1).
Row 6: P0 (1: 0: 0: 1: 1), (K1, P1) 5 (6: 8: 9: 10: 12) times, (K2, P2) twice, K2, P9, K2, P2, K2, P1, (K2, P2) 6 times, K2, P1, K2, P2, K2, P9,

K2, (P2, K2) twice, (P1, K1) 5 (6: 8: 9: 10: 12) times, P0 (1: 0: 0: 1: 1).
Row 7: K0 (1: 0: 0: 1: 1), (P1, K1) 5 (6: 8: 9: 10: 12) times, (P2, Tw2R) twice, P2, K9, P2, Tw2L, P2, yo, *sl 1, K1, psso, K2tog, (yfwd) twice, rep from * 5 times more, sl 1, K1, psso, K2tog, yo, P2, Tw2R, P2, K9, P2, (Tw2L, P2) twice, (K1, P1) 5 (6: 8: 9: 10: 12) times, K0 (1: 0: 0: 1: 1).
Row 8: K0 (1: 0: 0: 1: 1), (P1, K1) 5 (6: 8: 9: 10: 12) times, (K2, P2) twice, K2, P9, K2, P2, K3, *P2, (K1, P1) into double yfwd of previous row, rep from * 5 times more, P2, K3, P2, K2, P9, K2, (P2, K2) twice, (K1, P1) 5 (6: 8: 9: 10: 12) times, K0 (1: 0: 0: 1: 1).
These 8 rows form patt.
Cont in patt until back measures 41 (41: 42: 42: 42: 42) cm, ending with a WS row.

Shape armholes

Keeping patt correct, cast off 4 (4: 5: 5: 6: 6) sts at beg of next 2 rows.
90 (96: 100: 104: 108: 116) sts.
Dec 1 st at each end of next 3 (3: 5: 5: 7: 7) rows, then on foll 2 (4: 3: 4: 3: 5) alt rows.
80 (82: 84: 86: 88: 92) sts.
Cont straight until armhole measures approx 18 (19: 19: 20: 21: 22) cm, ending after patt row 4 (4: 4: 2: 2: 2) or 8 (8: 8: 6: 6: 6) and with a WS row.

Shape shoulders and back neck

Cast off 7 (7: 7: 7: 8: 8) sts at beg of next 2 rows.
66 (68: 70: 72: 72: 76) sts.
Next row (RS): Cast off 7 (7: 7: 7: 8: 8) sts, patt until there are 11 (11: 12: 12: 11: 13) sts on right needle and turn, leaving rem sts on a holder.
Work each side of neck separately.
Cast off 4 sts at beg of next row.
Cast off rem 7 (7: 8: 8: 7: 9) sts.
With RS facing, rejoin yarn and cast off centre 30 (32: 32: 34: 34: 34) sts, patt to end.
Complete to match first side, reversing shapings.

FRONT

Work as given for back until 12 (12: 12: 14: 14: 14) rows less have been worked than on back to start of shoulder shaping, ending after patt row 4 or 8 and with a WS row.

Shape front neck

Next row (RS): Patt 27 (27: 28: 29: 30: 32) sts and turn, leaving rem sts on a holder.
Work each side of neck separately.
Keeping patt correct, dec 1 st at neck edge of next 4 rows, then on foll 1 (1: 1: 2: 2: 2) alt rows, then on foll 4th row.
21 (21: 22: 22: 23: 25) sts.
Work 1 row, ending with a WS row.

Shape shoulder

Cast off 7 (7: 7: 7: 8: 8) sts at beg of next and foll alt row.
Work 1 row.
Cast off rem 7 (7: 8: 8: 7: 9) sts.
With RS facing, rejoin yarn and cast off centre 26 (28: 28: 28: 28: 28) sts, patt to end.
Complete to match first side, reversing shapings.

SLEEVES (both alike)

Cast on 48 (50: 52: 54: 56: 58) sts using 3¾mm (US 5) needles.
Row 1 (RS): P0 (0: 1: 0: 0: 0), K1 (2: 2: 0: 1: 2), *P2, K2, rep from * to last 3 (0: 1: 2: 3: 0) sts, P2 (0: 1: 2: 2: 0), K1 (0: 0: 0: 1: 0).
Row 2: K0 (0: 1: 0: 0: 0), P1 (2: 2: 0: 1: 2), *K2, P2, rep from * to last 3 (0: 1: 2: 3: 0) sts, K2 (0: 1: 2: 2: 0), P1 (0: 0: 0: 1: 0).
These 2 rows form rib.
Cont in rib for a further 21 rows, ending with a **RS** row.
Row 24 (WS): Rib 14 (15: 16: 17: 18: 19), M1, rib 20, M1, rib 14 (15: 16: 17: 18: 19).
50 (52: 54: 56: 58: 60) sts.
Change to 4½mm (US 7) needles.
Now work in patt as follows:
Row 1 (RS): P1 (0: 1: 0: 1: 0), (K1, P1) 2 (3: 3: 4: 4: 5) times, P2, Tw2R, P2, Tw2L, P3, (Tw2R, P2) 5 times, P1, Tw2R, P2, Tw2L, P2, (P1, K1) 2 (3: 3: 4: 4: 5) times, P1 (0: 1: 0: 1: 0).
Row 2: P1 (0: 1: 0: 1: 0), (K1, P1) 2 (3: 3: 4: 4: 5) times, (K2, P2) twice, K3, (P2, K2) 5 times, K1, (P2, K2) twice, (P1, K1) 2 (3: 3: 4: 4: 5) times, P1 (0: 1: 0: 1: 0).
Row 3: Inc in first st, K0 (1: 0: 1: 0: 1), (P1, K1) 2 (2: 3: 3: 4: 4) times, P2, Tw2R, P2, Tw2L, P2, *K2tog, (yfwd) twice, sl 1, K1, psso, rep from * 4 times more, P2, Tw2R, P2, Tw2L, P2, (K1, P1) 2 (2: 3: 3: 4: 4) times, K0 (1: 0: 1: 0: 1), inc in last st.
52 (54: 56: 58: 60: 62) sts.
Row 4: K0 (1: 0: 1: 0: 1), (P1, K1) 3 (3: 4: 4: 5: 5) times, (K2, P2) twice, K2, *P1, (K1, P1) into double yfwd of previous row, P1, rep from * 4 times more, K2, (P2, K2) twice, (K1, P1) 3 (3: 4: 4: 5: 5) times, K0 (1: 0: 1: 0: 1).

Row 5: P0 (1: 0: 1: 0: 1), (K1, P1) 3 (3: 4: 4: 5: 5) times, P2, Tw2R, P2, Tw2L, P2, K1, (P2, Tw2L) 4 times, P2, K1, P2, Tw2R, P2, Tw2L, P2, (P1, K1) 3 (3: 4: 4: 5: 5) times, P0 (1: 0: 1: 0: 1).
Row 6: P0 (1: 0: 1: 0: 1), (K1, P1) 3 (3: 4: 4: 5: 5) times, (K2, P2) twice, K2, P1, (K2, P2) 4 times, K2, P1, K2, (P2, K2) twice, (P1, K1) 3 (3: 4: 4: 5: 5) times, P0 (1: 0: 1: 0: 1).
Row 7: K0 (1: 0: 1: 0: 1), (P1, K1) 3 (3: 4: 4: 5: 5) times, P2, Tw2R, P2, Tw2L, P2, yo, *sl 1, K1, psso, K2tog, (yfwd) twice, rep from * 3 times more, sl 1, K1, psso, K2tog, yo, P2, Tw2R, P2, Tw2L, P2, (K1, P1) 3 (3: 4: 4: 5: 5) times, K0 (1: 0: 1: 0: 1).
Row 8: K0 (1: 0: 1: 0: 1), (P1, K1) 3 (3: 4: 4: 5: 5) times, (K2, P2) twice, K3, *P2, (K1, P1) into double yfwd of previous row, rep from * 3 times more, P2, K3, (P2, K2) twice, (K1, P1) 3 (3: 4: 4: 5: 5) times, K0 (1: 0: 1: 0: 1).
These 8 rows form patt and start sleeve shaping.
Cont in patt, shaping sides by inc 1 st at each end of 5th (5th: 7th: 7th: 5th: 5th) and 2 (0: 0: 0: 2: 1) foll 10th rows, then on every foll 12th row until there are 68 (70: 72: 72: 78: 80) sts, then on 0 (0: 0: 1: 0: 0) foll 14th row, taking inc sts into double moss st.
68 (70: 72: 74: 78: 80) sts.
Cont straight until sleeve measures 46 (47: 48: 49: 50: 51) cm, ending with a WS row.

Shape top

Keeping patt correct, cast off 4 (4: 5: 5: 6: 6) sts at beg of next 2 rows.
60 (62: 62: 64: 66: 68) sts.
Dec 1 st at each end of next 3 rows, then on foll alt row, then on 3 foll 4th rows.
46 (48: 48: 50: 52: 54) sts.
Work 1 row.
Dec 1 st at each end of next and every foll alt row until 38 sts rem, then on foll 5 rows, ending with a WS row.
Cast off rem 28 sts.

MAKING UP

Press all pieces with a warm iron over a damp cloth.
Join right shoulder seam using back stitch or mattress stitch if preferred.

Neckband

With RS facing and using 3¾mm (US 5) needles, pick up and knit 22 (22: 22: 25: 25: 25) sts down left side of front neck, 26 (28: 28: 28: 28: 28) sts from front, 22 (22: 22: 25: 25: 25) sts up right side of front neck, and 40 (42: 42: 44: 44: 44) sts from back.
110 (114: 114: 122: 122: 122) sts.
Row 1 (WS): K1, *K2, P2, rep from * to last st, P1.

Row 2: As row 1.
Last 2 rows form rib.
Cont in rib until neckband measures 9 cm, ending with a WS row.
Cast off in rib.
Join left shoulder and neckband seam. Join side seams. Join sleeve seams. Insert sleeves into armholes.

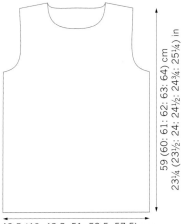

43.5 (46: 48.5: 51: 53.5: 57.5) cm
17¼ (18¼: 19¼: 20: 21: 22½) in

59 (60: 61: 62: 63: 64) cm
23¼ (23½: 24: 24½: 24¾: 25¼) in

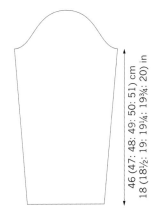

46 (47: 48: 49: 50: 51) cm
18 (18½: 19: 19¼: 19¾: 20) in

Recommendation ○○○
Please see pages 34 & 35 for photographs.

	XS	S	M	L	XL	XXL
To fit bust	**81**	**86**	**91**	**97**	**102**	**109** cm
	32	34	36	38	40	43 in

Rowan Cotton Glacé

	11	12	13	13	14	14 x 50gm

Photographed in Black

Needles
1 pair 2¾mm (no 12) (US 2) needles
1 pair 3¼mm (no 10) (US 3) needles
Cable needle

Buttons - 7

Tension
23 sts and 32 rows to 10 cm measured over pattern using 3¼mm (US 3) needles.

Special abbreviations
C4B = slip next 2 sts onto cable needle and leave at back of work, K2, then K2 from cable needle; **C4F** = slip next 2 sts onto cable needle and leave at front of work, K2, then K2 from cable needle; **C6B** = slip next 3 sts onto cable needle and leave at back of work, K3, then K3 from cable needle; **C6F** = slip next 3 sts onto cable needle and leave at front of work, K3, then K3 from cable needle.

Pattern note: When casting off across top of cables it is advisable to work "K2tog" (or "P2tog" on WS rows) at top of each cable to avoid edge becoming too wide. All sts counts given do NOT include these decreased sts but relate to the original number of sts.

EXHALE
FITTED CARDIGAN WITH SCULPTED CABLES

BACK
Cast on 118 (126: 134: 142: 150: 160) sts using 2¾mm (US 2) needles.
Row 1 (RS): P0 (0: 0: 0: 0: 1), (K2, P2) 4 (5: 6: 7: 8: 9) times, K3, (P2, K2) 6 times, (P2, K3) 6 times, (P2, K2) 6 times, P2, K3, (P2, K2) 4 (5: 6: 7: 8: 9) times, P0 (0: 0: 0: 0: 1).
Row 2: K0 (0: 0: 0: 0: 1), (P2, K2) 4 (5: 6: 7: 8: 9) times, P3, (K2, P2) 6 times, (K2, P3) 6 times, (K2, P2) 6 times, K2, P3, (K2, P2) 4 (5: 6: 7: 8: 9) times, K0 (0: 0: 0: 0: 1).
These 2 rows form rib.
Work in rib for a further 5 rows, ending with a **RS** row.
Row 8 (WS): K0 (0: 0: 0: 0: 1), (P2, K2tog) 3 (4: 5: 6: 7: 8) times, rib 5, M1P, rib 14, K2tog, rib 52, K2tog, rib 13, M1P, rib 6, (K2tog, P2) 3 (4: 5: 6: 7: 8) times, K0 (0: 0: 0: 1).
112 (118: 124: 130: 136: 144) sts.
Change to 3¼mm (US 3) needles.
Now work in patt as follows:
Row 1 (RS): K1 (0: 1: 0: 1: 1), (P1, K1) 5 (7: 8: 10: 11: 13) times, P2, C4B, *P2, C6B, (P1, K1) 4 times, P1, C6F, P2*, (C4B, C4F, P2) twice, C4B, C4F, rep from * to * once more, C4F, P2, (K1, P1) 5 (7: 8: 10: 11: 13) times, K1 (0: 1: 0: 1: 1).
Row 2: K1 (0: 1: 0: 1: 1), (P1, K1) 5 (7: 8: 10: 11: 13) times, K2, P4, *K2, P6, K2, (P1, K1) twice, P1, K2, P6, K2*, (P8, K2) twice, P8, rep from * to * once more, P4, K2, (K1, P1) 5 (7: 8: 10: 11: 13) times, K1 (0: 1: 0: 1: 1).
Row 3: P1 (0: 1: 0: 1: 1), (K1, P1) 5 (7: 8: 10: 11: 13) times, P2, K4, *P2, K6, P2, (K1, P1) twice, K1, P2, K6, P2*, (K8, P2) twice, K8, rep from * to * once more, K4, P2, (P1, K1) 5 (7: 8: 10: 11: 13) times, P1 (0: 1: 0: 1: 1).
Row 4: P1 (0: 1: 0: 1: 1), (K1, P1) 5 (7: 8: 10: 11: 13) times, K2, P4, *K2, P6, (K1, P1) 4 times, K1, P6, K2*, (P8, K2) twice, P8, rep from * to * once more, P4, K2, (P1, K1) 5 (7: 8: 10: 11: 13) times, P1 (0: 1: 0: 1: 1).
Row 5: K1 (0: 1: 0: 1: 1), (P1, K1) 5 (7: 8: 10: 11: 13) times, P2, C4F, *P2, C6B, (P1, K1) 4 times, P1, C6F, P2*, (C4F, C4B, P2) twice, C4F, C4B, rep from * to * once more, C4B, P2, (K1, P1) 5 (7: 8: 10: 11: 13) times, K1 (0: 1: 0: 1: 1).
Rows 6 to 8: As rows 2 to 4.
These 8 rows form patt.

Work in patt for a further 8 rows, ending with a WS row.
Counting in from both ends of last row, place a marker after 25th (28th: 31st: 34th: 37th: 41st) st in from ends of row, miss next 9 sts and place another marker – 4 markers in total and 44 sts between markers at centre of row.
Row 17 (RS): *Patt to marker, slip marker onto right needle, P2tog, patt to within 2 sts of next marker, P2tog tbl, slip marker onto right needle, rep from * once more, patt to end.
Noting there are now 2 sts less in double moss st between markers, work 7 rows.
Rep last 8 rows twice more.
100 (106: 112: 118: 124: 132) sts.
Row 41 (RS): *Patt to marker, slip marker onto right needle, P3tog, slip marker onto right needle, rep from * once more, patt to end.
96 (102: 108: 114: 120: 128) sts.
Noting that there is now just one st between markers and working this st in rev st st, work 17 rows.
Next row (RS): *Patt to marker, slip marker onto right needle, M1P, K1, M1P, slip marker onto right needle, rep from * once more, patt to end.
Now working sts between markers into patt as set previously, work 9 rows.
Next row (RS): *Patt to marker, slip marker onto right needle, M1P, patt to next marker, M1P, slip marker onto right needle, rep from * once more, patt to end.
Rep last 10 rows twice more.
112 (118: 124: 130: 136: 144) sts.
Cont straight until back measures 37 (37: 38: 38: 38: 38) cm, ending with a WS row.
Shape armholes
Keeping patt correct, cast off 5 (5: 6: 6: 7: 7) sts at beg of next 2 rows.
102 (108: 112: 118: 122: 130) sts.
Dec 1 st at each end of next 1 (3: 3: 5: 5: 7) rows, then on foll 4 (4: 5: 5: 6: 6) alt rows, then on foll 4th row. 90 (92: 94: 96: 98: 102) sts.
Cont straight until armhole measures 18 (19: 19: 20: 21: 22) cm, ending with a WS row.
Shape shoulders and back neck
Keeping patt correct, cast off 8 (8: 8: 8: 9: 9) sts at beg of next 2 rows (see pattern note).
74 (76: 78: 80: 80: 84) sts.

Next row (RS): Cast off 8 (8: 8: 8: 9: 9) sts, patt until there are 12 (12: 13: 13: 12: 14) sts on right needle and turn, leaving rem sts on a holder.
Work each side of neck separately.
Cast off 4 sts at beg of next row.
Cast off rem 8 (8: 9: 9: 8: 10) sts.
With RS facing, rejoin yarn and cast off centre 34 (36: 36: 38: 38: 38) sts, patt to end.
Complete to match first side, reversing shapings.

LEFT FRONT
Cast on 66 (70: 74: 78: 82: 87) sts using 2¾mm (US 2) needles.
Row 1 (RS): P0 (0: 0: 0: 0: 1), (K2, P2) 4 (5: 6: 7: 8: 9) times, K3, (P2, K2) 6 times, (P2, K3) 3 times, K8.
Row 2: K8, (P3, K2) 3 times, (P2, K2) 6 times, P3, (K2, P2) 4 (5: 6: 7: 8: 9) times, K0 (0: 0: 0: 0: 1).
These 2 rows set the sts – front opening edge 8 sts in g st with all other sts in rib.
Cont as set for a further 5 rows, ending with a **RS** row.
Row 8 (WS): K8, P1, M1P, rib 24, K2tog, rib 13, M1P, rib 6, (K2tog, P2) 3 (4: 5: 6: 7: 8) times, K0 (0: 0: 0: 0: 1).
64 (67: 70: 73: 76: 80) sts.
Change to 3¼mm (US 3) needles.
Now work in patt as follows:
Row 1 (RS): K1 (0: 1: 0: 1: 1), (P1, K1) 5 (7: 8: 10: 11: 13) times, P2, C4B, P2, C6B, (P1, K1) 4 times, P1, C6F, P2, C4B, C4F, P2, C4B, K8.
Row 2: K8, P4, K2, P8, K2, P6, K2, (P1, K1) twice, P1, K2, P6, K2, P4, K2, (K1, P1) 5 (7: 8: 10: 11: 13) times, K1 (0: 1: 0: 1: 1).
These 2 rows **set position** of patt as given for back with front opening edge 8 sts still worked in g st.
Keeping patt correct as now set, cont as follows:
Work in patt for a further 14 rows, ending with a WS row.
Counting in from end of last row, place a marker after 25th (28th: 31st: 34th: 37th: 41st) st in from end of row, miss next 9 sts and place another marker – 2 markers in total and 30 sts beyond marker at front opening edge.
Row 17 (RS): Patt to marker, slip marker onto right needle, P2tog, patt to within 2 sts of next marker, P2tog tbl, slip marker onto right needle, patt to end.
Noting there are now 2 sts less in double moss st between markers, work 7 rows.
Rep last 8 rows twice more.
58 (61: 64: 67: 70: 74) sts.

Row 41 (RS): Patt to marker, slip marker onto right needle, P3tog, slip marker onto right needle, patt to end.
56 (59: 62: 65: 68: 72) sts.
Noting that there is now just one st between markers and working this st in rev st st, work 17 rows.
Next row (RS): Patt to marker, slip marker onto right needle, M1P, K1, M1P, slip marker onto right needle, patt to end.
Now working sts between markers into patt as set previously, work 9 rows.
Next row (RS): Patt to marker, slip marker onto right needle, M1P, patt to next marker, M1P, slip marker onto right needle, patt to end.
Rep last 10 rows twice more.
64 (67: 70: 73: 76: 80) sts.
Cont straight until left front matches back to beg of armhole shaping, ending with a WS row.
Shape armhole
Keeping patt correct, cast off 5 (5: 6: 6: 7: 7) sts at beg of next row.
59 (62: 64: 67: 69: 73) sts.
Work 1 row.
Dec 1 st at armhole edge of next 1 (3: 3: 5: 5: 7) rows, then on foll 4 (4: 5: 5: 6: 6) alt rows, then on foll 4th row.
53 (54: 55: 56: 57: 59) sts.
Cont straight until 24 (24: 24: 26: 26: 26) rows less have been worked than on back to start of shoulder shaping, ending with a WS row.
Shape front neck
Next row (RS): Patt 34 (34: 35: 36: 37: 39) sts and turn, leaving rem 19 (20: 20: 20: 20: 20) sts on a holder (for neckband).
Keeping patt correct, dec 1 st at neck edge of next 6 rows, then on foll 2 (2: 2: 3: 3: 3) alt rows, then on 2 foll 4th rows.
24 (24: 25: 25: 26: 28) sts.
Work 5 rows, ending with a WS row.
Shape shoulder
Cast off 8 (8: 8: 8: 9: 9) sts at beg of next and foll alt row.
Work 1 row.
Cast off rem 8 (8: 9: 9: 8: 10) sts.
Mark positions for 7 buttons along left front opening edge – first button to come level with row 37 (this is 29th row in patt after rib), last button to come level with start of neck shaping, and rem 5 buttons evenly spaced between.

RIGHT FRONT
Cast on 66 (70: 74: 78: 82: 87) sts using 2¾mm (US 2) needles.
Row 1 (RS): K8, (K3, P2) 3 times, (K2, P2) 6 times, K3, (P2, K2) 4 (5: 6: 7: 8: 9) times, P0 (0: 0: 0: 0: 1).

Row 2: K0 (0: 0: 0: 0: 1), (P2, K2) 4 (5: 6: 7: 8: 9) times, P3, (K2, P2) 6 times, (K2, P3) 3 times, K8.
These 2 rows set the sts – front opening edge 8 sts in g st with all other sts in rib.
Cont as set for a further 5 rows, ending with a **RS** row.
Row 8 (WS): K0 (0: 0: 0: 0: 1), (P2, K2tog) 3 (4: 5: 6: 7: 8) times, rib 6, M1P, rib 13, K2tog, rib 24, M1P, P1, K8.
64 (67: 70: 73: 76: 80) sts.
Change to 3¼mm (US 3) needles.
Now work in patt as follows:
Row 1 (RS): K8, C4F, P2, C4B, C4F, P2, C6B, (P1, K1) 4 times, P1, C6F, P2, C4F, P2, (K1, P1) 5 (7: 8: 10: 11: 13) times, K1 (0: 1: 0: 1: 1).
Row 2: K1 (0: 1: 0: 1: 1), (P1, K1) 5 (7: 8: 10: 11: 13) times, K2, P4, K2, P6, K2, (P1, K1) twice, P1, K2, P6, K2, P8, K2, P4, K8.
These 2 rows **set position** of patt as given for back with front opening edge 8 sts still worked in g st.
Keeping patt correct as now set, cont as follows:
Work in patt for a further 14 rows, ending with a WS row.
Counting in from beg of last row, place a marker after 25th (28th: 31st: 34th: 37th: 41st) st in from beg of row, miss next 9 sts and place another marker – 2 markers in total and 30 sts beyond marker at front opening edge.
Row 17 (RS): Patt to marker, slip marker onto right needle, P2tog, patt to within 2 sts of next marker, P2tog tbl, slip marker onto right needle, patt to end.
Noting there are now 2 sts less in double moss st between markers, work 7 rows.
Row 25: As row 17.
Work 3 rows, ending with a WS row.
Row 29 (RS): K2, K2tog tbl, yfwd (to make a buttonhole), patt to end.
Making a further 5 buttonholes in this way to correspond with positions marked for buttons on left front and noting that no further reference will be made to buttonholes, complete to match left front, reversing shapings and working first row of front neck shaping as follows:
Shape front neck
Next row (RS): K2, K2tog tbl, yfwd (to make 7th buttonhole), K5, K2tog, K4, (K2tog) twice, K0 (1: 1: 1: 1: 1) and slip these 16 (17: 17: 17: 17: 17) sts onto a holder (for neckband), patt to end.
34 (34: 35: 36: 37: 39) sts.

SLEEVES (both alike)

Cast on 70 (72: 76: 78: 80: 86) sts using 2¾mm (US 2) needles.

Row 1 (RS): K2 (3: 1: 2: 3: 2), (P2, K2) 3 (3: 4: 4: 4: 5) times, (P2, K3) 8 times, P2, (K2, P2) 3 (3: 4: 4: 4: 5) times, K2 (3: 1: 2: 3: 2).

Row 2: P2 (3: 1: 2: 3: 2), (K2, P2) 3 (3: 4: 4: 4: 5) times, (K2, P3) 8 times, K2, (P2, K2) 3 (3: 4: 4: 4: 5) times, P2 (3: 1: 2: 3: 2).

These 2 rows form rib.

Work in rib for a further 13 rows, ending with a **RS** row.

Row 16 (WS): P2 (3: 1: 2: 3: 2), (K2tog, P2) 3 (3: 4: 4: 4: 5) times, K2, P1, M1P, P2, (K2, P3) 6 times, K2, P1, M1P, P2, K2, (P2, K2tog) 3 (3: 4: 4: 4: 5) times, P2 (3: 1: 2: 3: 2). 66 (68: 70: 72: 74: 78) sts.

Change to 3¼mm (US 3) needles.

Now work in patt as follows:

Row 1 (RS): K1 (0: 1: 0: 1: 1), (P1, K1) 5 (6: 6: 7: 7: 8) times, P2, C4B, (P2, C4B, C4F) 3 times, P2, C4F, P2, (K1, P1) 5 (6: 6: 7: 7: 8) times, K1 (0: 1: 0: 1: 1).

Row 2: K1 (0: 1: 0: 1: 1), (P1, K1) 5 (6: 6: 7: 7: 8) times, K2, P4, (K2, P8) 3 times, K2, P4, K2, (K1, P1) 5 (6: 6: 7: 7: 8) times, K1 (0: 1: 0: 1: 1).

Row 3: Inc in first st, P0 (1: 0: 1: 0: 0), (K1, P1) 5 (5: 6: 6: 7: 8) times, P2, K4, (P2, K8) 3 times, P2, K4, P2, (P1, K1) 5 (5: 6: 6: 7: 8) times, P0 (1: 0: 1: 0: 0), inc in last st. 68 (70: 72: 74: 76: 80) sts.

Row 4: P0 (1: 0: 1: 0: 0), (K1, P1) 6 (6: 7: 7: 8: 9) times, K2, P4, (K2, P8) 3 times, K2, P4, K2, (P1, K1) 6 (6: 7: 7: 8: 9) times, P0 (1: 0: 1: 0: 0).

Row 5: K0 (1: 0: 1: 0: 0), (P1, K1) 6 (6: 7: 7: 8: 9) times, P2, C4F, (P2, C4F, C4B) 3 times, P2, C4B, P2, (K1, P1) 6 (6: 7: 7: 8: 9) times, K0 (1: 0: 1: 0: 0).

Row 6: K0 (1: 0: 1: 0: 0), (P1, K1) 6 (6: 7: 7: 8: 9) times, K2, P4, (K2, P8) 3 times, K2, P4, K2, (K1, P1) 6 (6: 7: 7: 8: 9) times, K0 (1: 0: 1: 0: 0).

Row 7: P0 (1: 0: 1: 0: 0), (K1, P1) 6 (6: 7: 7: 8: 9) times, P2, K4, (P2, K8) 3 times, P2, K4, P2, (P1, K1) 6 (6: 7: 7: 8: 9) times, P0 (1: 0: 1: 0: 0).

Row 8: P0 (1: 0: 1: 0: 0), (K1, P1) 6 (6: 7: 7: 8: 9) times, K2, P4, (K2, P8) 3 times, K2, P4, K2, (P1, K1) 6 (6: 7: 7: 8: 9) times, P0 (1: 0: 1: 0: 0).

These 8 rows form patt and start sleeve shaping. Keeping patt correct as now set, cont as follows:

Inc 1 st at each end of 7th (7th: 7th: 7th: 7th: 9th) and every foll 12th (12th: 12th: 14th: 12th: 14th) row to 80 (80: 78: 86: 90: 88) sts, then on every foll – (14th: 14th: -: -: 16th) row until there are - (82: 84: -: -: 92) sts, taking inc sts into double moss st.

Cont straight until sleeve measures 33 (34: 35: 36: 37: 38) cm, ending with a WS row.

Shape top

Keeping patt correct, cast off 5 (5: 6: 6: 7: 7) sts at beg of next 2 rows.

70 (72: 72: 74: 76: 78) sts.

Dec 1 st at each end of next 3 rows, then on foll 2 alt rows, then on 4 foll 4th rows.

52 (54: 54: 56: 58: 60) sts.

Work 1 row.

Dec 1 st at each end of next and every foll alt row until 46 sts rem, then on foll 7 rows, ending with a WS row.

Cast off rem 32 sts.

MAKING UP

Press all pieces with a warm iron over a damp cloth. Join both shoulder seams using back stitch or mattress stitch if preferred.

Neckband

With RS facing and using 2¾mm (US 2) needles, slip 16 (17: 17: 17: 17: 17) sts from right front holder onto right needle, rejoin yarn and pick up and knit 21 (21: 21: 23: 23: 23) sts up right side of front neck, 30 (32: 32: 34: 34: 34) sts from back, and 21 (21: 21: 23: 23: 23) sts down left side of front neck, then K across 19 (20: 20: 20: 20: 20) sts on left front holder as follows: K0 (1: 1: 1: 1: 1), (K2tog) twice, K4, K2tog, K9.

104 (108: 108: 114: 114: 114) sts.

Work in g st for a further 8 rows, ending with a **RS** row.

Cast off knitwise (on **WS**).

Join side seams. Join sleeve seams. Insert sleeves into armholes. Sew on buttons.

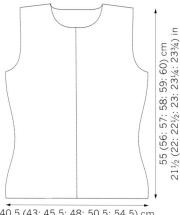

40.5 (43: 45.5: 48: 50.5: 54.5) cm
16 (17: 18: 19: 20: 21½) in

55 (56: 57: 58: 59: 60) cm
21½ (22: 22½: 23: 23¼: 23¾) in

33 (34: 35: 36: 37: 38) cm
13 (13½: 13¾: 14¼: 14½: 15) in

Recommendation ◌◌
Please see pages 32 & 33 for photographs.

	XS	S	M	L	XL	XXL	
To fit bust	**81**	**86**	**91**	**97**	**102**	**109**	cm
	32	34	36	38	40	43	in

Rowan Handknit Cotton

| | 6 | 7 | 7 | 8 | 8 | 9 | x 50gm |

Photographed in Black

Needles
1 pair 3¼mm (no 10) (US 3) needles
1 pair 3¾mm (no 9) (US 5) needles
1 pair 7mm (no 2) (US 10½) needles

Tension
15 sts and 22 rows to 10 cm measured over pattern using a combination of 3¾mm (US 5) and 7mm (US 10½) needles.

SUNSET
LOW KEY REVERSIBLE TOP

BACK
Cast on 83 (88: 93: 98: 103: 110) sts using 3¼mm (US 3) needles.
Row 1 (RS): P0 (0: 0: 0: 0: 1), K3, *P2, K3, rep from * to last 0 (0: 0: 0: 0: 1) st, P0 (0: 0: 0: 0: 1).
Row 2: K0 (0: 0: 0: 0: 1), P3, *K2, P3, rep from * to last 0 (0: 0: 0: 0: 1) st, K0 (0: 0: 0: 0: 1).
These 2 rows form rib.
Work in rib for a further 15 rows, ending with a **RS** row.
Row 18 (WS): K0 (0: 0: 0: 0: 1), P3, *K2tog, P3, rep from * to last 0 (0: 0: 0: 0: 1) st, K0 (0: 0: 0: 0: 1). 67 (71: 75: 79: 83: 89) sts.
Using a 3¾mm (US 5) needle, K one row, dec 1 st at centre of row. 66 (70: 74: 78: 82: 88) sts.
Now work in patt as follows:
Row 1 (WS): Using a 7mm (US 10½) needle, purl.
Row 2: Using a 3¾mm (US 5) needle, knit.
These 2 rows form patt.
Cont in patt until back measures 53.5 (54.5: 55.5: 56.5: 57.5: 58.5) cm, ending with a WS row.
Shape back neck
Keeping patt correct, cont as folls:
Next row (RS): K18 (19: 21: 22: 24: 27) and turn, leaving rem sts on a holder.
Work each side of neck separately.
Dec 1 st at neck edge of next 3 rows, ending with a WS row. 15 (16: 18: 19: 21: 24) sts.
Shape shoulder
Cast off 4 (5: 5: 6: 6: 7) sts at beg of next and foll alt row and at same time dec 1 st at neck edge of next and foll alt row.
Work 1 row.
Cast off rem 5 (4: 6: 5: 7: 8) sts.
With RS facing, rejoin yarn and cast off centre 30 (32: 32: 34: 34: 34) sts, K to end.
Complete to match first side, reversing shapings.

FRONT
Work as for back until 54 (54: 54: 56: 56: 56) rows less have been worked than on back to start of shoulder shaping, ending with a WS row.
Divide for front neck
Keeping patt correct, cont as folls:
Next row (RS): K28 (30: 32: 34: 36: 39), K2tog tbl, K3 and turn, leaving rem sts on a holder. 32 (34: 36: 38: 40: 43) sts.
Work each side of neck separately.

Working all neck decreases as set by last row, dec 1 st at neck edge of 2nd and foll 12 (14: 14: 15: 15: 15) alt rows, then on 5 (4: 4: 4: 4: 4) foll 4th rows, then on foll 6th row.
13 (14: 16: 17: 19: 22) sts.
Work 1 row, ending with a WS row.
Shape shoulder
Cast off 4 (5: 5: 6: 6: 7) sts at beg of next and foll alt row.
Work 1 row.
Cast off rem 5 (4: 6: 5: 7: 8) sts.
With RS facing, rejoin yarn to sts on holder, K3, K2tog, K to end. 32 (34: 36: 38: 40: 43) sts.
Complete to match first side, reversing shapings.

MAKING UP
Press all pieces with a warm iron over a damp cloth.
Using back stitch or mattress stitch if preferred, join right shoulder seam.
Neckband
With RS facing and using 3¼mm (US 3) needles, pick up and knit 61 (61: 61: 65: 65: 65) sts down left side of front neck, place marker on needle, 60 (60: 60: 64: 64: 64) sts up right side of front neck, and 49 (49: 49: 53: 53: 53) sts from back neck. 170 (170: 170: 182: 182: 182) sts.
Row 1 (WS): P2, *inc knitwise in next st, P3, rep from * to within 3 sts of marker, inc knitwise in next st, P2tog, slip marker onto right needle, P2tog tbl, inc knitwise in next st, **P3, inc knitwise in next st, rep from ** to last 2 sts, P2. 210 (210: 210: 225: 225: 225) sts.
Row 2: K2, *P2, K3, rep from * to within 3 sts of marker, P1, P2tog, slip marker onto right needle, P2tog tbl, P1, **K3, P2, rep from ** to last 2 sts, K2.
Last row sets position of rib as given for back.
Keeping rib correct and working all decreases as set by last 2 rows, cont as folls:
Work in rib for a further 4 rows, dec 1 st at each side of marker on every row and ending with a **RS** row. 200 (200: 200: 215: 215: 215) sts.
Cast off in rib (on **WS**), still dec either side of marker as before.
Join left shoulder and neckband seam. Mark points along side seam edges 22 (23: 23: 24: 25: 26) cm either side of shoulder seams (to denote base of armhole openings).

Continued on next page...

Recommendation ○

Please see pages 44 & 45 for photographs.

	XS	S	M	L	XL	XXL	
To fit bust	81	86	91	97	102	109	cm
	32	34	36	38	40	43	in

Rowan Handknit Cotton and Summerlite 4 ply

Handknit Cotton

	8	9	9	10	10	11	x 50gm

Summerlite 4 ply

	4	5	5	5	6	6	x 50gm

Photographed in Handknit Cotton in Ballet Pink and Summerlite 4 ply in Blossom

Needles

1 pair 5½mm (no 5) (US 9) needles
1 pair 6½mm (no 3) (US 10½) needles

Tension

14 sts and 18 rows to 10 cm measured over stocking stitch using 6½mm (US 10½) needles and one strand each of Handknit Cotton and Summerlite 4 ply held together.

SUGAR

UNDERSTATED SWEATER WORKED IN TWO YARNS

Special note: We found it preferable to knit the two yarns together from separate balls rather than winding them together.

BACK

Cast on 67 (71: 75: 79: 83: 87) sts using 6½mm (US 10½) needles and one strand each of Handknit Cotton and Summerlite 4 ply held together.

Row 1 (RS): K to last st, pick up loop lying between needles and place this loop on right needle (**Note:** This loop does **NOT** count as a st), with yarn still at back (WS) of work slip last st **purlwise**.

Row 2: P tog the first st and the picked-up loop, P to last st, pick up loop lying between needles and place this loop on right needle (**Note:** This loop does **NOT** count as a st), slip last st **knitwise**.

Row 3: K tog **tbl** the first st and the picked-up loop, K to last st, pick up loop lying between needles and place this loop on right needle (**Note:** This loop does **NOT** count as a st), slip last st **purlwise**.

Last 2 rows set the sts – slip st edging at both ends of rows and all other sts in st st.

Cont as now set until back measures 12 cm, ending with a WS row.

Place markers at both ends of last row (to denote top of side seam openings).

Now working **all** sts in st st, cont as follows:

Cont straight until back measures 41 (41: 42:

42: 42: 42) cm, ending with a WS row.

Shape armholes

Cast off 3 (3: 4: 4: 5: 5) sts at beg of next 2 rows. 61 (65: 67: 71: 73: 77) sts.

Next row (RS): K3, K2tog, K to last 5 sts, K2tog tbl, K3.

Next row: P3, P2tog tbl, P to last 5 sts, P2tog, P3.

Working all armhole decreases as set by last 2 rows, dec 1 st at each end of next and foll 1 (2: 2: 4: 4: 5) alt rows, then on foll 4th row. 51 (53: 55: 55: 57: 59) sts.

Cont straight until armhole measures 18 (19: 19: 20: 21: 22) cm, ending with a WS row.

Shape shoulders and back neck

Cast off 4 (4: 4: 4: 4: 5) sts at beg of next 2 rows. 43 (45: 47: 47: 49: 49) sts.

Next row (RS): Cast off 4 (4: 4: 4: 4: 5) sts, K until there are 8 (8: 9: 8: 9: 8) sts on right needle and turn, leaving rem sts on a holder. Work each side of neck separately.

Cast off 4 sts at beg of next row.

Cast off rem 4 (4: 5: 4: 5: 4) sts.

With RS facing, rejoin yarns and cast off centre 19 (21: 21: 23: 23: 23) sts, K to end.

Complete to match first side, reversing shapings.

FRONT

Work as given for back until 6 (6: 6: 8: 8: 8) rows less have been worked than on back to start of shoulder shaping, ending with a WS row.

SUNSET – Continued from previous page.

Armhole borders (both alike)

With RS facing and using 3¼mm (US 3) needles, pick up and knit 97 (101: 101: 105: 109: 113) sts evenly along armhole row-end edge between markers.

Row 1 (WS): P2, *inc knitwise in next st, P3, rep from * to last 3 sts, inc knitwise in next st, P2. 121 (126: 126: 131: 136: 141) sts.

Row 2: K2, *P2, K3, rep from * to last 4 sts, P2, K2.

Last row sets position of rib as given for back.

Keeping rib correct as now set, work in rib for a further 10 rows, ending with a **RS** row.

Cast off in rib (on **WS**).

Join side and armhole border seams

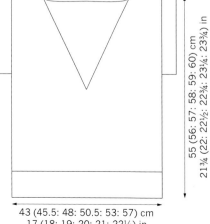

43 (45.5: 48: 50.5: 53: 57) cm
17 (18: 19: 20: 21: 22½) in

55 (56: 57: 58: 59: 60) cm
21¾ (22: 22½: 22¾: 23¼: 23¾) in

Shape front neck

Next row (RS): K17 (17: 18: 18: 19: 20) and turn, leaving rem sts on a holder.
Work each side of neck separately.
Dec 1 st at neck edge of next 4 rows, then on foll 0 (0: 0: 1: 1: 1) alt rows.
13 (13: 14: 13: 14: 15) sts.
Work 1 row, ending with a WS row.

Shape shoulder

Cast off 4 (4: 4: 4: 4: 5) sts at beg of next and foll alt row **and at same time** dec 1 st at neck edge of next row.
Work 1 row.
Cast off rem 4 (4: 5: 4: 5: 4) sts.
With RS facing, slip centre 17 (19: 19: 19: 19: 19) sts onto a holder (for neckband). Rejoin yarns and K to end.
Complete to match first side, reversing shapings.

SLEEVES (both alike)

Cast on 30 (32: 34: 34: 36: 38) sts using 6½mm (US 10½) needles and one strand each of Handknit Cotton and Summerlite 4 ply held together.
Starting with a K row, work in st st throughout as follows:
Work 16 rows, ending with a WS row.
Next row (RS): K3, M1, K to last 3 sts, M1, K3.
Working all sleeve increases as set by last row, inc 1 st at each end of 8th (10th: 10th: 8th: 8th: 8th) and 0 (0: 0: 2: 1: 1) foll 8th rows, then on 5 (5: 4: 4: 5: 5) foll 10th rows, then on 0 (0: 1: 0: 0: 0) foll 12th rows.
44 (46: 48: 50: 52: 54) sts.
Cont straight until sleeve measures 46 (47: 48: 49: 50: 51) cm, ending with a WS row.

Shape top

Cast off 3 (3: 4: 4: 5: 5) sts at beg of next 2 rows. 38 (40: 40: 42: 42: 44) sts.
Dec 1 st at each end of next and foll alt row, then on 2 foll 4th rows. 30 (32: 32: 34: 34: 36) sts.
Work 1 row.
Dec 1 st at each end of next and every foll alt row until 26 sts rem, then on foll 3 rows, ending with a WS row.
Cast off rem 20 sts.

MAKING UP

Press all pieces with a warm iron over a damp cloth. Join right shoulder seam using back stitch or mattress stitch if preferred.

Neckband

With RS facing, using 5½mm (US 9) needles and one strand each of Handknit Cotton and Summerlite 4 ply held together, pick up and knit 11 (11: 11: 13: 13: 13) sts down left side of front neck, K across 17 (19: 19: 19: 19: 19) sts on front holder, pick up and knit 10 (10: 10: 13: 13: 13) sts up right side of front neck, and 27 (29: 29: 32: 32: 32) sts from back. 65 (69: 69: 77: 77: 77) sts.
Row 1 (WS): P2, *inc knitwise in next st, P3, rep from * to last 3 sts, inc knitwise in next st, P2. 81 (86: 86: 96: 96: 96) sts.
Row 2: K2, *P2, K3, rep from * to last 4 sts, P2, K2.
Row 3: P2, *K2, P3, rep from * to last 4 sts, K2, P2.
Last 2 rows form rib.
Cont in rib until neckband measures 9 cm, ending with a **RS** row.
Cast off in rib (on **WS**).
Join left shoulder and neckband seam. Join side seams. Join sleeve seams. Insert sleeves into armholes.

59 (60: 61: 62: 63: 64) cm
23¼ (23¾: 24: 24½: 24¾: 25¼) in

48 (50.5: 53: 55.5: 58: 62) cm
19 (20: 21: 22: 23: 24½) in

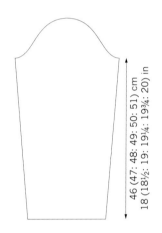

46 (47: 48: 49: 50: 51) cm
18 (18½: 19: 19¼: 19¾: 20) in

SIRAN

NEAT CHEVRON STRIPED SWEATER

	XS	S	M	L	XL	XXL	
To fit bust	81	86	91	97	102	109	cm
	32	34	36	38	40	43	in

Rowan Summerlite DK

A Black

	2	2	3	3	3	4	x 50gm

B Pink Powder

	5	5	5	6	6	7	x 50gm

One-colour version

	6	7	8	8	9	10	x 50gm

Needles
1 pair 2¾mm (no 12) (US 2) needles
1 pair 3¼mm (no 10) (US 3) needles
2¾mm (no 12) (US 2) circular needle

Tension
30 sts and 29 rows to 10 cm measured over
pattern using 3¼mm (US 3) needles.

Pattern note: Take care to ensure each dec
of patt is matched by an inc. If there are
insufficient sts to work both, work end sts of
rows in st st.

Special abbreviations
sL2togK = slip 2 sts as though to K2tog; **p2sso**
= pass 2 slipped sts over.

One-colour version
Work as given for two-colour version but using
same colour throughout.

BACK
Cast on 99 (107: 113: 119: 125: 135) sts
using 2¾mm (US 2) needles and yarn A.
Row 1 (RS): K1 (0: 0: 1: 0: 0), P2 (2: 0: 2: 1: 1),
*K3, P2, rep from * to last 1 (0: 3: 1: 4: 4) sts,
K1 (0: 3: 1: 3: 3), P0 (0: 0: 0: 1: 1).
Row 2: P1 (0: 0: 1: 0: 0), K2 (2: 0: 2: 1: 1),
*P3, K2, rep from * to last 1 (0: 3: 1: 4: 4) sts,
P1 (0: 3: 1: 3: 3), K0 (0: 0: 0: 1: 1).
These 2 rows form rib.
Cont in rib for a further 21 rows, ending with a
RS row.
Row 24 (WS): P1 (0: 0: 1: 0: 0), K1 (2: 0: 1:
1: 1), (M1, K1) 1 (0: 0: 1: 0: 0) times, *P3, K1,
M1, K1, rep from * to last 1 (5: 3: 1: 4: 4) sts,
P1 (3: 3: 1: 3: 3), K0 (2: 0: 0: 1: 1).
119 (127: 135: 143: 149: 161) sts.
Change to 3¼mm (US 3) needles.
Now work in patt as follows:
Row 1 (RS): K5 (4: 1: 5: 3: 2), (sl 1, K1, psso,
K4, yfwd, K1) 1 (0: 1: 1: 0: 1) times, *yfwd, K4,
sL2togK, K1, p2sso, K4, yfwd, K1, rep from * to
last 11 (3: 7: 11: 2: 8) sts, (yfwd, K4, K2tog)
1 (0: 1: 1: 0: 1) times, K5 (3: 1: 5: 2: 2).
Row 2: Purl.
These 2 rows form patt.
Keeping patt correct throughout, cont as
follows:
Work 4 rows, ending with a WS row.
Join in yarn B.
Using yarn B, work 6 rows.
Using yarn A, work 8 rows.
Using yarn B, work 6 rows.
Using yarn A, work 8 rows.
Break off yarn A and complete back using yarn
B **only**.
Cont in patt until back measures 29 (29: 30:
30: 30: 30) cm, ending with a WS row.
Shape armholes
Keeping patt correct, cast off 4 (4: 5: 5: 6: 6) sts
at beg of next 2 rows.
111 (119: 125: 133: 137: 149) sts.
Dec 1 st at each end of next 3 (5: 5: 7: 7: 9)
rows, then on foll 2 (3: 4: 5: 5: 7) alt rows, then
on foll 4th row. 99 (101: 105: 107: 111: 115) sts.
Cont straight until armhole measures 17 (18:
18: 19: 20: 21) cm, ending with a WS row.
Shape shoulders and back neck
Cast off 9 (9: 10: 10: 10: 11) sts at beg of next
2 rows. 81 (83: 85: 87: 91: 93) sts.

Next row (RS): Cast off 9 (9: 10: 10: 10: 11) sts,
patt until there are 13 (13: 13: 13: 15: 15) sts
on right needle and turn, leaving rem sts on a
holder.
Work each side of neck separately.
Cast off 4 sts at beg of next row.
Cast off rem 9 (9: 9: 9: 11: 11) sts.
With RS facing, rejoin yarn and cast off centre
37 (39: 39: 41: 41: 41) sts, patt to end.
Complete to match first side, reversing
shapings.

FRONT
Work as given for back until 23 rows less have
been worked than on back to start of armhole
shaping, ending with a **RS** row.
Divide for front opening
Next row (WS): P55 (59: 63: 67: 70: 76) and
slip these sts onto a holder (for right side of
front), cast off next 9 sts purlwise, P to end.
55 (59: 63: 67: 70: 76) sts.
Work each side of neck separately.
Next row (RS): Patt to last 7 sts, yfwd, K4,
K2tog, K1.
Keeping patt correct as set by last row, cont as
follows:
Cont straight until left side of front matches
back to start of armhole shaping, ending with
a WS row.
Shape armhole
Keeping patt correct, cast off 4 (4: 5: 5: 6: 6) sts
at beg of next row. 51 (55: 58: 62: 64: 70) sts.
Work 1 row.
Dec 1 st at armhole edge of next 3 (5: 5: 7: 7: 9)
rows, then on foll 2 (3: 4: 5: 5: 7) alt rows, then
on foll 4th row.
45 (46: 48: 49: 51: 53) sts.
Cont straight until 20 (20: 20: 22: 22: 22) rows
less have been worked than on back to start of
shoulder shaping, ending with a WS row.
Shape front neck
Next row (RS): Patt 36 (36: 38: 39: 41: 43) sts,
cast off rem 9 (10: 10: 10: 10: 10) sts.
Break yarn.
Rejoin yarn with **WS** facing and cont as follows:
Keeping patt correct, dec 1 st at neck edge of
next 6 rows, then on foll 1 (1: 1: 2: 2: 2) alt
rows, then on 2 foll 4th rows.
27 (27: 29: 29: 31: 33) sts.
Work 3 rows, ending with a WS row.

Shape shoulder

Cast off 9 (9: 10: 10: 10: 11) sts at beg of next and foll alt row.

Work 1 row.

Cast off rem 9 (9: 9: 9: 11: 11) sts.

With RS facing, rejoin yarn to sts on holder and cont as follows:

Next row (RS): K1, sl 1, K1, psso, K4, yfwd, patt to end.

Complete to match first side, reversing shapings and working first row of neck shaping as folls:

Shape front neck

Next row (RS): Cast off 9 (10: 10: 10: 10: 10) sts, patt to end. 36 (36: 38: 39: 41: 43) sts.

SLEEVES (both alike)

Cast on 71 (73: 75: 77: 79: 81) sts using 2¾mm (US 2) needles and yarn B.

Row 1 (RS): K2 (0: 0: 0: 1: 2), P2 (0: 1: 2: 2: 2), *K3, P2, rep from * to last 2 (3: 4: 0: 1: 2) sts, K2 (3: 3: 0: 1: 2), P0 (0: 1: 0: 0: 0).

Row 2: P2 (0: 0: 0: 1: 2), K2 (0: 1: 2: 2: 2), *P3, K2, rep from * to last 2 (3: 4: 0: 1: 2) sts, P2 (3: 3: 0: 1: 2), K0 (0: 1: 0: 0: 0).

These 2 rows form rib.

Cont in rib for a further 7 rows, ending with a **RS** row.

Row 10 (WS): P2 (0: 0: 0: 1: 2), K1 (0: 1: 2: 1: 1), (M1, K1) 1 (0: 0: 0: 1: 1) times, *P3, K1, M1, K1, rep from * to last 2 (3: 4: 5: 1: 2) sts, P2 (3: 3: 3: 1: 2), K0 (0: 1: 2: 0: 0).

85 (87: 89: 91: 95: 97) sts.

Change to 3¼mm (US 3) needles.

Now work in patt as follows:

Row 1 (RS): K0 (1: 2: 3: 5: 1), (sl 1, K1, psso, K4, yfwd, K1) 1 (1: 1: 1: 1: 0) times, *yfwd, K4, sL2togK, K1, p2sso, K4, yfwd, K1, rep from * to last 6 (7: 8: 9: 11: 0) sts, (yfwd, K4, K2tog) 1 (1: 1: 1: 1: 0) times, K0 (1: 2: 3: 5: 0).

Row 2: Purl.

These 2 rows form patt.

Keeping patt correct throughout, cont as folls:

Inc 1 st at each end of next and foll 8th row, taking inc sts into st st.

89 (91: 93: 95: 99: 101) sts.

Cont straight until sleeve measures 10 (10: 10: 11: 11: 11) cm, ending with a WS row.

Shape top

Keeping patt correct, cast off 4 (4: 5: 5: 6: 6) sts at beg of next 2 rows. 81 (83: 83: 85: 87: 89) sts.

Dec 1 st at each end of next 3 rows, then on foll 2 alt rows, then on foll 4th row.

69 (71: 71: 73: 75: 77) sts.

Work 1 row.

Dec 1 st at each end of next and every foll alt row until 59 sts rem, then on foll 5 rows, ending with a WS row. 49 sts.

Cast off 3 sts at beg of next 2 rows.

Cast off rem 43 sts.

MAKING UP

Press all pieces with a warm iron over a damp cloth.

Join both shoulder seams using back stitch or mattress stitch if preferred.

Front bands (both alike)

With RS facing, using 2¾mm (US 2) needles and yarn B, pick up and knit 41 (43: 43: 43: 47: 49) sts evenly along one side of front opening, between cast-off sts at base of opening and cast-off sts at start of neck shaping.

Row 1 (WS): K1, *P1, K1, rep from * to end.

Row 2: As row 1.

Last 2 rows form moss st.

Work in moss st for a further 12 rows, ending with a **RS** row.

Cast off in moss st (on **WS**).

Neckband

With RS facing, using 2¾mm (US 2) circular needle and yarn B, starting and ending at cast-off edges of front bands, pick up and knit 8 sts across top of right front band, 26 (27: 27: 29: 29: 29) sts up right side of front neck, 40 (42: 42: 44: 44: 44) sts from back, 26 (27: 27: 29: 29: 29) sts down left side of front neck, and 8 sts across top of left front band.

108 (112: 112: 118: 118: 118) sts.

Work in g st for 8 rows, ending with a **RS** row.

Cast off knitwise (on **WS**).

Lay right front band over left front band and neatly sew row-end edges to cast-off sts at base of opening. Join side seams. Join sleeve seams. Insert sleeves into armholes.

47 (48: 49: 50: 51: 52) cm
18½ (19: 19¼: 19¾: 20: 20½) in

39.5 (43: 45: 47.5: 49.5: 53.5) cm
15½ (17: 17¾: 18¾: 19½: 21) in

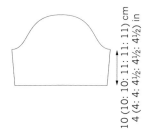

10 (10: 10: 11: 11: 11) cm
4 (4: 4: 4½: 4½: 4½) in

SUNRISE
GENEROUS OPENWORK SWEATER WITH CABLES

Recommendation ○○
Please see pages 40 & 41 for photographs.

	XS	S	M	L	XL	XXL	
To fit bust	**81**	**86**	**91**	**97**	**102**	**109**	**cm**
	32	34	36	38	40	43	in

Rowan Handknit Cotton
14 15 16 17 18 19 x 50gm
Photographed in Slate

Needles
1 pair 3mm (no 11) (US 2/3) needles
1 pair 3¾mm (no 9) (US 5) needles
Cable needle

Tension
18 sts and 28 rows to 10 cm measured over mesh pattern using 3¾mm (US 5) needles.

Special abbreviations
C4B = slip next 3 sts onto cable needle and leave at back of work, K1, then K3 from cable needle; **C4F** = slip next st onto cable needle and leave at front of work, K3, then K1 from cable needle; **C6B** = slip next 3 sts onto cable needle and leave at back of work, K3, then K3 from cable needle; **C6F** = slip next 3 sts onto cable needle and leave at front of work, K3, then K3 from cable needle; **C8B** = slip next 4 sts onto cable needle and leave at back of work, K4, then K4 from cable needle; **C8F** = slip next 4 sts onto cable needle and leave at front of work, K4, then K4 from cable needle.

BACK
Cast on 123 (127: 131: 137: 141: 147) sts using 3mm (US 2/3) needles.
Row 1 (RS): K2 (0: 1: 0: 1: 0), P2 (1: 2: 1: 2: 1), (K3, P2) 4 (5: 5: 6: 6: 7) times, (K2, P2) 4 times, (K3, P2) 9 times, K2, (P2, K2) 3 times, (P2, K3) 4 (5: 5: 6: 6: 7) times, P2 (1: 2: 1: 2: 1), K2 (0: 1: 0: 1: 0).
Row 2: P2 (0: 1: 0: 1: 0), K2 (1: 2: 1: 2: 1), (P3, K2) 4 (5: 5: 6: 6: 7) times, (P2, K2) 4 times, (P3, K2) 9 times, P2, (K2, P2) 3 times, (K2, P3) 4 (5: 5: 6: 6: 7) times, K2 (1: 2: 1: 2: 1), P2 (0: 1: 0: 1: 0).
These 2 rows form rib.
Cont in rib for a further 23 rows, ending with a **RS** row.
Row 26 (WS): Rib 4 (6: 8: 11: 13: 16), P2tog, rib 11, inc in next st, rib 12, K2tog, rib 11, inc in next st, rib 11, (P2tog, rib 3) twice, P2tog, rib 11, inc in next st, rib 12, K2tog, rib 11, inc in next st, rib 11, P2tog, rib 5 (7: 9: 12: 14: 17).
120 (124: 128: 134: 138: 144) sts.
Change to 3¾mm (US 5) needles.
Now work in patt as follows:
Row 1 (RS): K1 (3: 1: 0: 2: 1), *K2tog, (yfwd) twice, sl 1, K1, psso*, rep from * to * 1 (1: 2: 3: 3: 4) times more, K2, **P2, C4F, K1, C4B, P2, place marker on needle, K6, P1, K6, place another marker on needle, P2, C4F, K1, C4B, P2**, K2, rep from * to * 4 times, K2, rep from ** to ** once more, K2, rep from * to * 2 (2: 3: 4: 4: 5) times, K1 (3: 1: 0: 2: 1).
Row 2: P1 (3: 1: 0: 2: 1), *P1, (P1, K1) into double yfwd of previous row, P1*, rep from * to * 1 (1: 2: 3: 3: 4) times more, P2, **K2, P9, K2, slip marker from left needle to right needle, P6, K1, P6, slip marker from left needle to right needle, K2, P9, K2**, P2, rep from * to * 4 times, P2, rep from ** to ** once more, P2, rep from * to * 2 (2: 3: 4: 4: 5) times, P1 (3: 1: 0: 2: 1).
Row 3: K3 (1: 3: 2: 0: 3), *K2tog, (yfwd) twice, sl 1, K1, psso*, rep from * to * 1 (2: 2: 3: 4: 4) times more, **P2, K9, P2, slip marker from left needle to right needle, C6F, P1, C6B, slip marker from left needle to right needle, P2, K9, P2**, rep from * to * 5 times, rep from ** to ** once more, rep from * to * 2 (3: 3: 4: 5: 5) times, K3 (1: 3: 2: 0: 3).

Row 4: P3 (1: 3: 2: 0: 3), *P1, (P1, K1) into double yfwd of previous row, P1*, rep from * to * 1 (2: 2: 3: 4: 4) times more, **K2, P9, K2, slip marker from left needle to right needle, P6, K1, P6, slip marker from left needle to right needle, K2, P9, K2**, rep from * to * 5 times, rep from ** to ** once more, rep from * to * 2 (3: 3: 4: 5: 5) times, P3 (1: 3: 2: 0: 3).
These 4 rows set the sts – sts at side seam edges and at centre in mesh patt, cables next to these sts and then cables between each pair of markers.
Keeping sts correct as now set **EXCEPT** between each pair of markers, cont as follows:
Row 5 (RS): (Patt to marker, slip marker from left needle to right needle, K6, P1, K6, slip marker from left needle to right needle) twice, patt to end.
Row 6: (Patt to marker, slip marker from left needle to right needle, P6, K1, P6, slip marker from left needle to right needle) twice, patt to end.
Rep last 2 rows 3 times more.
Row 13 (RS): (Patt to marker, slip marker from left needle to right needle, C6F, P1, C6B, slip marker from left needle to right needle) twice, patt to end.
Rep row 6 once more, then rep rows 5 and 6, 5 times more, ending with a WS row.
Row 25 (RS): (Patt to marker, slip marker from left needle to right needle, slip next 3 sts onto cable needle and leave at front of work, K2, inc in next st, then work across 3 sts on cable needle as follows: inc in first st, K2, P1, slip next 3 sts onto cable needle and leave at back of work, K2, inc in next st, then work across 3 sts on cable needle as follows: inc in first st, K2, slip marker from left needle to right needle) twice, patt to end.
128 (132: 136: 142: 146: 152) sts.
Row 26 (WS): (Patt to marker, slip marker from left needle to right needle, P8, K1, P8, slip marker from left needle to right needle) twice, patt to end.
Row 27: (Patt to marker, slip marker from left needle to right needle, K8, P1, K8, slip marker from left needle to right needle) twice, patt to end.
Rows 28 to 37: As rows 26 and 27, 5 times.
Row 38: As row 26.

Row 39: (Patt to marker, slip marker from left needle to right needle, C8F, P1, C8B, slip marker from left needle to right needle) twice, patt to end.

Rows 26 to 39 form patt for rest of back.

Cont in patt until back measures 29 (29: 30: 30: 30: 30) cm, ending with a WS row.

Shape armholes

Keeping patt correct, cast off 4 sts at beg of next 2 rows.

120 (124: 128: 134: 138: 144) sts.

Cont straight until armhole measures 21 (22: 22: 23: 24: 25) cm, ending with a WS row.

Shape shoulders

Keeping patt correct, cast off 3 (3: 3: 3: 3: 4) sts at beg of next 16 (16: 14: 10: 6: 16) rows, then – (-: 4: 4: 4: -) sts at beg of foll – (-: 2: 6: 10: -) rows.

72 (76: 78: 80: 80: 80) sts.

Shape back neck

Next row (RS): Cast off 3 (3: 4: 4: 4: 4) sts, patt until there are 7 (8: 8: 8: 8: 8) sts on right needle and turn, leaving rem sts on a holder.

Work each side of neck separately.

Cast off 4 sts at beg of next row.

Cast off rem 3 (4: 4: 4: 4: 4) sts.

With RS facing, rejoin yarn and cast off centre 52 (54: 54: 56: 56: 56) sts, patt to end.

Complete to match first side, reversing shapings.

FRONT

Work as given for back until 4 (4: 4: 6: 6: 6) rows less have been worked than on back to start of shoulder shaping, ending with a WS row.

Shape front neck

Next row (RS): Patt 39 (40: 42: 45: 47: 50) sts and turn, leaving rem sts on a holder.

Work each side of neck separately.

Keeping patt correct, dec 1 st at neck edge of next 3 (3: 3: 4: 4: 4) rows.

36 (37: 39: 41: 43: 46) sts.

Work 0 (0: 0: 1: 1: 1) row, ending with a WS row.

Shape shoulder

Cast off 3 (3: 3: 3: 3: 4) sts at beg of next and foll 8 (8: 6: 4: 2: 8) alt rows, then – (-: 4: 4: 4: -) sts at beg of foll – (-: 2: 4: 6: -) alt rows **and at same time** dec 1 st at neck edge of next and foll 4 alt rows, then on foll 4th row..

Work 1 row.

Cast off rem 3 (4: 4: 4: 4: 4) sts.

With RS facing, rejoin yarn and cast off centre 42 (44: 44: 44: 44: 44) sts, patt to end.

Complete to match first side, reversing shapings.

SLEEVES (both alike)

Cast on 46 (48: 50: 52: 54: 56) sts using 3mm (US 2/3) needles.

Row 1 (RS): K0 (0: 0: 1: 0: 0), P0 (1: 2: 2: 0: 1), *K2, P2, rep from * to last 2 (3: 0: 1: 2: 3) sts, K2 (2: 0: 1: 2: 2), P0 (1: 0: 0: 0: 1).

Row 2: P0 (0: 0: 1: 0: 0), K0 (1: 2: 2: 0: 1), *P2, K2, rep from * to last 2 (3: 0: 1: 2: 3) sts, P2 (2: 0: 1: 2: 2), K0 (1: 0: 0: 0: 1).

These 2 rows form rib.

Cont in rib for a further 16 rows, ending with a WS row.

Change to 3¾mm (US 5) needles.

Now work in patt as follows:

Row 1 (RS): Inc in first st, K2 (1: 2: 1: 2: 1), *K2tog, (yfwd) twice, sl 1, K1, psso, rep from * to last 3 (2: 3: 2: 3: 2) sts, K2 (1: 2: 1: 2: 1), inc in last st.

48 (50: 52: 54: 56: 58) sts.

Row 2: P2 (3: 2: 3: 2: 3), *P1, (P1, K1) into double yfwd of previous row, P1, rep from * to last 2 (3: 2: 3: 2: 3) sts, P2 (3: 2: 3: 2: 3).

Row 3: Inc in first st, K1 (0: 1: 0: 1: 0), *K2tog, (yfwd) twice, sl 1, K1, psso, rep from * to last 2 (1: 2: 1: 2: 1) sts, K1 (0: 1: 0: 1: 0), inc in last st.

50 (52: 54: 56: 58: 60) sts.

Row 4: P1 (2: 1: 2: 1: 2), *P1, (P1, K1) into double yfwd of previous row, P1, rep from * to last 1 (2: 1: 2: 1: 2) sts, P1 (2: 1: 2: 1: 2).

These 4 rows form mesh patt and start sleeve shaping.

Cont as set, shaping sides by inc 1 st at each end of next and foll 5 (6: 5: 6: 6: 7) alt rows, then on 4 foll 4th rows, then on 4 foll 6th rows, taking inc sts into st st until there are sufficient to take into patt.

78 (82: 82: 86: 88: 92) sts.

Cont straight until sleeve measures 47 (48: 49: 50: 51: 52) cm, ending with a WS row.

Shape top

Keeping patt correct, cast off 7 (8: 8: 8: 8: 9) sts at beg of next 2 (8: 8: 4: 2: 8) rows, then 8 (-: -: 9: 9: -) sts at beg of foll 6 (-: -: 4: 6: -) rows.

Cast off rem 16 (18: 18: 18: 18: 20) sts.

MAKING UP

Press all pieces with a warm iron over a damp cloth.

Join right shoulder seam using back stitch or mattress stitch if preferred.

Neckband

With RS facing and using 3mm (US 2/3) needles, pick up and knit 20 (21: 21: 25: 25: 25) sts down left side of front neck, 42 (44: 44: 44: 44: 44) sts from front,

20 (20: 20: 24: 24: 24) sts up right side of front neck, and 65 (67: 67: 69: 69: 69) sts from back.

147 (152: 152: 162: 162: 162) sts.

Row 1 (WS): K2, *P3, K2, rep from * to end.

Row 2: P2, *K3, P2, rep from * to end.

Last 2 rows form rib.

Cont in rib for a further 6 rows, ending with a **RS** row.

Cast off in rib (on **WS**).

Join left shoulder and neckband seam. Join side seams. Join sleeve seams, leaving seam open for 2 cm at upper edge. Insert sleeves into armholes, matching last 2 cm of sleeve seam to cast-off sts of armhole and shaped cast-off edge of sleeve to armhole row-end edge.

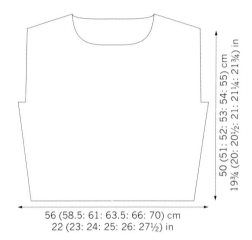

56 (58.5: 61: 63.5: 66: 70) cm
22 (23: 24: 25: 26: 27½) in

50 (51: 52: 53: 54: 55) cm
19¾ (20: 20½: 21: 21¼: 21¾) in

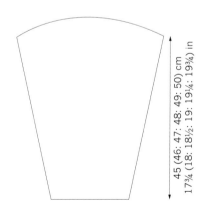

45 (46: 47: 48: 49: 50) cm
17¾ (18: 18½: 19: 19¼: 19¾) in

SWEET

PRETTY REVERSIBLE SWEATER WITH SIDE VENTS

Recommendation ◯◯
Please see pages 42 & 52 for photographs.

	XS	S	M	L	XL	XXL	
To fit bust	**81**	**86**	**91**	**97**	**102**	**109**	**cm**
	32	34	36	38	40	43	in

Rowan Kidsilk Haze

| | 4 | 5 | 5 | 5 | 6 | 6 | x 25gm |

Photographed in Grace

Needles
1 pair 2¾mm (no 12) (US 2) needles
1 pair 3¼mm (no 10) (US 3) needles

Tension
25 sts and 34 rows to 10 cm measured over
stocking stitch using 3¼mm (US 3) needles.

BACK
Cast on 102 (108: 112: 118: 124: 134)
sts using 2¾mm (US 2) needles and yarn
DOUBLE.
Break off one strand of yarn and complete
back using SINGLE strand of yarn.
Work in g st for 16 rows, ending with a WS row.
Change to 3¼mm (US 3) needles.
Next row (RS): Knit.
Next row: K6, P to last 6 sts, K6.
Rep last 2 rows until back measures 10 cm,
ending with a WS row.
Place markers at both ends of last row (to
denote top of side seam openings).
Now working **all** sts in st st, cont as follows:
Cont straight until back measures 40 (40: 41:
41: 41: 41) cm, ending with a WS row.
Shape armholes
Cast off 4 (4: 5: 5: 6: 6) sts at beg of next
2 rows.
94 (100: 102: 108: 112: 122) sts.
Dec 1 st at each end of next 1 (3: 3: 5: 5: 7)
rows, then on foll 4 (4: 4: 3: 4: 5) alt rows, then
on foll 4th row. 82 (84: 86: 90: 92: 96) sts.
Cont straight until armhole measures
12.5 (13.5: 13.5: 14.5: 15.5: 16.5) cm, ending
with a WS row.
Shape back neck
Next row (RS): K21 (21: 22: 23: 24: 26) and
turn, leaving rem sts on a holder.
Work each side of neck separately.
Cast off 3 sts at beg of next row, then 2 sts at
beg of foll 3 alt rows. 12 (12: 13: 14: 15: 17) sts.
Work 2 rows, ending with a WS row.
Dec 1 st at neck edge of next row.
11 (11: 12: 13: 14: 16) sts.
Work 5 rows, ending with a WS row.
Shape shoulder
Cast off 5 (5: 6: 6: 7: 8) sts at beg of next row.
Work 1 row.
Cast off rem 6 (6: 6: 7: 7: 8) sts.
With RS facing, rejoin yarn and cast off centre
40 (42: 42: 44: 44: 44) sts, K to end.
Complete to match first side, reversing
shapings.

FRONT
Work as given for back until 24 rows less have
been worked than on back to start of armhole
shaping, ending with a WS row.

Divide for front neck
Next row (RS): K47 (50: 52: 55: 58: 63),
K2tog tbl, K2 and turn, leaving rem sts on a
holder.
50 (53: 55: 58: 61: 66) sts.
Work each side of neck separately.
Work 1 row.
Next row (RS): K to last 4 sts, K2tog tbl, K2.
Working all neck decreases as set by last row,
dec 1 st at neck edge of 2nd and foll 9 alt
rows. 39 (42: 44: 47: 50: 55) sts.
Work 1 row, ending with a WS row.
Shape armhole
Cast off 4 (4: 5: 5: 6: 6) sts at beg and dec 1 st
at end of next row. 34 (37: 38: 41: 43: 48) sts.
Work 1 row.
Dec 1 st at armhole edge of next 1 (3: 3: 5: 5: 7)
rows, then on foll 4 (4: 4: 3: 4: 5) alt rows, then
on foll 4th row **and at same time** dec 1 st at
neck edge of next and foll 6 (7: 7: 7: 8: 9) alt
rows. 21 (21: 22: 24: 24: 25) sts.
Dec 1 st at neck edge **only** on 2nd and foll
5 (4: 4: 5: 2: 0) alt rows, then on 3 (4: 4: 4: 6: 7)
foll 4th rows, then on foll 6th row.
11 (11: 12: 13: 14: 16) sts.
Cont straight until front matches back to start
of shoulder shaping, ending with a WS row.
Shape shoulder
Cast off 5 (5: 6: 6: 7: 8) sts at beg of next row.
Work 1 row.
Cast off rem 6 (6: 6: 7: 7: 8) sts.
With RS facing, rejoin yarn, K2, K2tog, K to end.
50 (53: 55: 58: 61: 66) sts.
Work 1 row.
Next row (RS): K2, K2tog, K to end.
Working all neck decreases as set by last
row, complete to match first side, reversing
shapings.

SLEEVES (both alike)
Cast on 61 (63: 65: 69: 71: 73) sts using
2¾mm (US 2) needles and yarn DOUBLE.
Break off one strand of yarn and complete
back using SINGLE strand of yarn.
Work in g st for 16 rows, ending with a WS row.
Change to 3¼mm (US 3) needles.
Starting with a K row, work in st st throughout
as follows:
Work 2 rows, ending with a WS row.
Next row (RS): K3, M1, K to last 3 sts, M1, K3.

Working all sleeve increases as set by last row, inc 1 st at each end of 16th (16th: 16th: 22nd: 18th: 18th) and every foll 16th (16th: 16th: 22nd: 18th: 18th) row to 73 (71: 71: 77: 79: 79) sts, then on every foll – (18th: 18th: 24th: 20th: 20th) row until there are - (75: 77: 79: 83: 85) sts.

Cont straight until sleeve measures 32 (33: 34: 35: 36: 37) cm, ending with a WS row.

Shape top

Cast off 4 (4: 5: 5: 6: 6) sts at beg of next 2 rows. 65 (67: 67: 69: 71: 73) sts.

Dec 1 st at each end of next 3 rows, then on foll alt row, then on 5 foll 4th rows.
47 (49: 49: 51: 53: 55) sts.

Work 1 row.

Dec 1 st at each end of next and every foll alt row until 43 sts rem, then on foll 9 rows, ending with a WS row.

Cast off rem 25 sts.

MAKING UP

Press all pieces with a warm iron over a damp cloth.

Join right shoulder seam using back stitch or mattress stitch if preferred.

Neckband

With RS facing and using 2¾mm (US 2) needles, pick up and knit 71 (74: 74: 76: 79: 82) sts down left side of front neck, place marker on needle, pick up and knit 71 (74: 74: 76: 79: 82) sts up right side of front neck, 18 sts down right side of back neck, 40 (42: 42: 44: 44: 44) sts from back, and 18 sts up left side of back neck. 218 (226: 226: 232: 238: 244) sts.

Row 1 (WS): Knit.

Row 2: K to within 2 sts of marker, K2tog tbl, slip marker onto right needle, K2tog, K to end.

Rep last 2 rows 3 times more, ending with a **RS** row.
210 (218: 218: 224: 230: 236) sts.

Join in second strand of yarn.

Using yarn DOUBLE, cast off knitwise (on **WS**).

Join left shoulder and neckband seam. Join side seams, leaving seams open below markers (for side seam openings). Join sleeve seams. Insert sleeves into armholes.

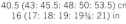

40.5 (43: 45.5: 48: 50: 53.5) cm
16 (17: 18: 19: 19¾: 21) in

57 (58: 59: 60: 61: 62) cm
22½ (23: 23¾: 23¾: 24: 24½) in

32 (33: 34: 35: 36: 37) cm
12½ (13: 13½: 13¾: 14¼: 14½) in

Recommendation ◑◐

Please see pages 46 & 47 for photographs.

	XS	S	M	L	XL	XXL	
To fit bust	**81**	**86**	**91**	**97**	**102**	**109**	cm
	32	34	36	38	40	43	in

Rowan Summerlite DK

| | 7 | 8 | 8 | 9 | 9 | 10 | x 50gm |

Photographed in Silvery Blue

Needles

1 pair 2¾mm (no 12) (US 2) needles
1 pair 3¼mm (no 10) (US 3) needles

Buttons - 6

Tension

26 sts and 52 rows to 10 cm measured over garter stitch using 2¾mm (US 2) needles. 16 sts and 36 rows to 10 cm measured over main pattern using 3¼mm (US 3) needles.

GLIMPSE

PRETTY CARDIGAN IN AN OPENWORK FABRIC

BACK

Cast on 104 (110: 118: 124: 130: 140) sts using 2¾mm (US 2) needles.
Work in g st for 14 rows, ending with a WS row.
Now work in lower patt as follows:
Row 1 (RS): Knit.
Row 2: K7, yfrn, P2tog, *yrn, P2tog, rep from * to last 7 sts, K7.
Rows 3 and 4: As row 2.
Rows 5 to 10: Knit.
Last 10 rows form lower patt.
Work in lower patt for a further 40 rows, ending with a WS row.
Place markers at both ends of last row (to denote top of side seam opening).
Change to 3¼mm (US 3) needles.
Next row (RS): K4 (5: 4: 4: 5: 5), (K2tog, K1, K2tog) 19 (20: 22: 23: 24: 26) times, K5 (5: 4: 5: 5: 5). 66 (70: 74: 78: 82: 88) sts.
Now work in main patt as follows:
Row 1 (WS): P1 (1: 1: 1: 1: 2), *yrn, P2tog, rep from * to last 1 (1: 1: 1: 1: 2) sts, P1 (1: 1: 1: 1: 2).
Row 2: As row 1.
These 2 rows form main patt.
Cont in main patt until back measures 39 (39: 40: 40: 40: 40) cm, ending with a WS row.
Shape armholes
Keeping patt correct, cast off 4 (4: 4: 4: 4: 5) sts at beg of next 2 rows.
58 (62: 66: 70: 74: 78) sts.
Dec **2** sts at each end of next and foll 0 (0: 1: 1: 2: 2) alt rows, then on 0 (1: 1: 1: 1: 1) foll 4th row.
54 (54: 54: 58: 58: 62) sts.
Cont straight until armhole measures 18 (19: 19: 20: 21: 22) cm, ending with a WS row.
Shape shoulders and back neck
Cast off 5 sts at beg of next 2 rows.
44 (44: 44: 48: 48: 52) sts.
Next row (RS): Cast off 5 sts, patt until there are 8 (8: 8: 8: 8: 10) sts on right needle and turn, leaving rem sts on a holder.
Work each side of neck separately.
Cast off 4 sts at beg of next row.
Cast off rem 4 (4: 4: 4: 4: 6) sts.
With RS facing, rejoin yarn and cast off centre 18 (18: 18: 22: 22: 22) sts, patt to end.
Complete to match first side, reversing shapings.

LEFT FRONT

Cast on 59 (63: 67: 69: 73: 77) sts using 2¾mm (US 2) needles.
Work in g st for 14 rows, ending with a WS row.
Now work in lower patt as follows:
Row 1 (RS): Knit.
Row 2: K8, yfrn, P2tog, *yrn, P2tog, rep from * to last 7 sts, K7.
Row 3: K7, yfrn, P2tog, *yrn, P2tog, rep from * to last 8 sts, K8.
Row 4: As row 2.
Rows 5 to 10: Knit.
Last 10 rows form lower patt.
Work in lower patt for a further 40 rows, ending with a WS row.
Place a marker at side edge of last row (to denote top of side seam opening).
Change to 3¼mm (US 3) needles.
Next row (RS): K6 (5: 4: 6: 5: 6), (K2tog, K1) 0 (0: 0: 0: 0: 1) times, (K2tog, K1, K2tog) 9 (10: 11: 11: 12: 12) times, K8.
41 (43: 45: 47: 49: 52) sts.
Now work in main patt as follows:
Row 1 (WS): K8, yfrn, P2tog, *yrn, P2tog, rep from * to last 1 (1: 1: 1: 1: 2) sts, P1 (1: 1: 1: 1: 2).
Row 2: P1 (1: 1: 1: 1: 2), *yrn, P2tog, rep from * to last 8 sts, K8.
These 2 rows set the sts – front opening edge 8 sts in g st with all other sts in main patt as given for back.
Cont as now set until left front matches back to start of armhole shaping, ending with a WS row.
Shape armhole
Keeping patt correct, cast off 4 (4: 4: 4: 4: 5) sts at beg of next row. 37 (39: 41: 43: 45: 47) sts.
Work 1 row.
Dec **2** sts at armhole edge of next and foll 0 (0: 1: 1: 2: 2) alt rows, then on 0 (1: 1: 1: 1: 1) foll 4th row. 35 (35: 35: 37: 37: 39) sts.
Cont straight until 22 (22: 22: 26: 26: 26) rows less have been worked than on back to start of shoulder shaping, ending with a WS row.
Shape front neck
Next row (RS): Patt 22 (22: 22: 24: 24: 26) sts and turn, leaving rem 13 sts on a holder (for neckband).
Work 1 row, ending with a WS row.
Dec **2** sts at neck edge of next and foll alt row, then on 1 (1: 1: 2: 2: 2) foll 4th rows, then on foll 6th row. 14 (14: 14: 14: 14: 16) sts.
Work 7 rows, ending with a WS row.

Shape shoulder

Cast off 5 sts at beg of next and foll alt row.
Work 1 row.

Cast off rem 4 (4: 4: 4: 4: 6) sts.

Mark positions for 6 buttons along left front
opening edge – first button to come level with
first RS row of main patt, last button to come
just above neck shaping, and rem 4 buttons
evenly spaced between.

RIGHT FRONT

Cast on 59 (63: 67: 69: 73: 77) sts using
2¾mm (US 2) needles.

Work in g st for 14 rows, ending with a WS row.
Now work in lower patt as follows:

Row 1 (RS): Knit.

Row 2: K7, yfrn, P2tog, *yrn, P2tog, rep from *
to last 8 sts, K8.

Row 3: K8, yfrn, P2tog, *yrn, P2tog, rep from *
to last 7 sts, K7.

Row 4: As row 2.

Rows 5 to 10: Knit.

Last 10 rows form lower patt.

Work in lower patt for a further 40 rows, ending
with a WS row.

Place a marker at side edge of last row (to
denote top of side seam opening).

Change to 3¼mm (US 3) needles.

Next row (RS): K8, (K2tog, K1, K2tog)
9 (10: 11: 11: 12: 12) times, (K1, K2tog)
0 (0: 0: 0: 0: 1) times, K6 (5: 4: 6: 5: 6).
41 (43: 45: 47: 49: 52) sts.

Now work in main patt as follows:

Row 1 (WS): P1 (1: 1: 1: 1: 2), *yrn, P2tog, rep
from * to last 8 sts, K8.

Row 2: K3, K2tog, yfwd (to make a buttonhole),
K3, yfrn, P2tog, *yrn, P2tog, rep from * to last
1 (1: 1: 1: 1: 2) sts, P1 (1: 1: 1: 1: 2).

These 2 rows set the sts – front opening edge
8 sts in g st with all other sts in main patt as
given for back.

Making a further 4 buttonholes as set by last
row to correspond with positions marked
for buttons on left front and noting that no
further reference will be made to buttonholes,
complete to match left front, reversing
shapings and working first row of neck shaping
as follows:

Shape front neck

Next row (RS): K13 and slip these 13 sts onto
a holder (for neckband), patt to end.
22 (22: 22: 24: 24: 26) sts.

SLEEVES (both alike)

Cast on 62 (66: 66: 68: 72: 74) sts using
2¾mm (US 2) needles.

Work in g st for 15 rows, ending with a **RS** row.

Row 16 (WS): P1, *yrn, P2tog, rep from * to
last st, P1.

Rows 17 and 18: As row 16.

Work in g st for a further 6 rows, ending with a
WS row.

Change to 3¼mm (US 3) needles.

Next row (RS): K1 (0: 0: 1: 0: 1), (K2tog, K1)
20 (22: 22: 22: 24: 24) times, K1 (0: 0: 1: 0: 1).
42 (44: 44: 46: 48: 50) sts.

Now work in main patt as follows:

Row 1 (WS): P1, *yrn, P2tog, rep from * to last st, P1.

Row 2: As row 1.

These 2 rows form main patt.

Work in patt for a further 27 rows, ending with
a WS row.

Row 30 (RS): Inc **twice** in first st (by working
into front, back and front again), patt to last st,
inc **twice** in last st. 46 (48: 48: 50: 52: 54) sts.
Work 23 (25: 27: 29: 31: 33) rows.

Next row (RS): As row 30.
50 (52: 52: 54: 56: 58) sts.

Cont straight until sleeve measures 33 (34: 35:
36: 37: 38) cm, ending with a WS row.

Shape top

Keeping patt correct, cast off 4 (4: 4: 4: 4: 5) sts
at beg of next 2 rows. 42 (44: 44: 46: 48: 48) sts.
Dec **2** sts at each end of 3rd (5th: 5th: 5th:
7th: 7th) and 0 (0: 0: 1: 1: 2) foll 10th rows,
then on 3 (3: 3: 2: 2: 1) foll 8th rows, then on
foll 6th row, then on foll 4th row, then on foll alt
row. 14 (16: 16: 18: 20: 20) sts.

Work 1 row, ending with a WS row.

Cast off **loosely**.

MAKING UP

Press all pieces with a warm iron over a damp cloth.
Join both shoulder seams using back stitch or
mattress stitch if preferred.

Neckband

With RS facing and using 2¾mm (US 2)
needles, slip 13 sts from right front holder
onto right needle, rejoin yarn and pick up and
knit 26 (26: 26: 29: 29: 29) sts up right side
of front neck, 40 (40: 40: 46: 46: 46) sts from
back, and 26 (26: 26: 29: 29: 29) sts down left
side of front neck, then K across 13 sts on left
front holder. 118 (118: 118: 130: 130: 130) sts.

Next row (WS): Knit.

Next row: K3, K2tog, yfwd (to make 6th
buttonhole), K to end.

Work in g st for a further 6 rows, ending with a
RS row.

Cast off knitwise (on **WS**).

Join side seams, leaving side seams open
below markers on back and fronts. Join sleeve
seams. Insert sleeves into armholes. Sew on
buttons.

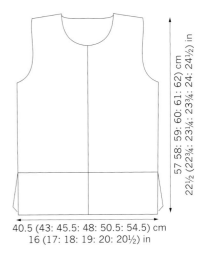

57 58: 59: 60: 61: 62) cm
22½ (22¾: 23¼: 23¾: 24: 24½) in

40.5 (43: 45.5: 48: 50.5: 54.5) cm
16 (17: 18: 19: 20: 20½) in

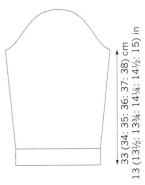

33 (34: 35: 36: 37: 38) cm
13 (13½: 13¾: 14¼: 14½: 15) in

Recommendation ○○

Please see pages 48 & 49 for photographs.

	XS	S	M	L	XL	XXL	
To fit bust	**81**	**86**	**91**	**97**	**102**	**109**	**cm**
	32	34	36	38	40	43	in

Rowan Kidsilk Haze

	5	6	6	7	7	8	x 25gm

Photographed in Aura

Needles

1 pair 3mm (no 11) (US 2/3) needles
1 pair 4mm (no 8) (US 6) needles
1 pair 8mm (no 0) (US 11) needles

Tension

12 sts and 19 rows to 10 cm measured over stocking stitch using a combination of 4mm (US 6) and 8mm (US 11) needles and yarn DOUBLE.

Special note: We found it preferable to knit the two yarns together from separate balls rather than winding them together.

BLUR

OFF THE SHOULDER SWEATER WITH ALTERNATE NECKLINE

WIDE NECK SWEATER

BACK and FRONT (both alike)

Cast on 116 (120: 128: 132: 140: 148) sts using 3mm (US 2/3) needles and yarn DOUBLE.
Break off one strand of yarn and continue using SINGLE strand of yarn as follows:
Work in g st for 20 rows, ending with a WS row.
Join in second strand of yarn and now using yarn DOUBLE throughout, cont as follows:
Next row (RS): Using 4mm (US 6) needle, *K2tog, rep from * to end.
58 (60: 64: 66: 70: 74) sts.
Now work in patt as follows:
Row 1 (WS): Using 8mm (US 11) needle, purl.
Row 2: Using 4mm (US 6) needle, knit.
Last 2 rows form patt.
Cont in patt until work measures 37 (37: 38: 38: 38: 38) cm, ending with a WS row.
Place markers at both ends of last row (to denote base of armhole openings).**
Cont straight until work measures 12 (13: 13: 14: 15: 16) cm **from markers**, ending with a WS row.

Shape neck

Next row (RS): K15 (16: 18: 19: 21: 23) and turn, leaving rem sts on a holder.
Work each side of neck separately.
Cast off 3 sts at beg of next row.
12 (13: 15: 16: 18: 20) sts.
Dec 1 st at neck edge of next 5 rows, then on foll 2 (2: 2: 3: 3: 3) alt rows. 5 (6: 8: 8: 10: 12) sts.
Work 1 row, ending with a WS row.

Shape shoulder

Cast off 2 (3: 4: 4: 5: 6) sts at beg of next row.
Work 1 row.
Cast off rem 3 (3: 4: 4: 5: 6) sts.
With RS facing, rejoin yarn DOUBLE, cast off centre 28 sts **loosely**, K to end.
15 (16: 18: 19: 21: 23) sts.
Complete to match first side, reversing shapings.

SLEEVES (both alike)

Cast on 50 (54: 58: 58: 62: 62) sts using 3mm (US 2/3) needles and yarn DOUBLE.
Break off one strand of yarn and continue using SINGLE strand of yarn as follows:
Work in g st for 20 rows, ending with a WS row.

Join in second strand of yarn and now using yarn DOUBLE throughout, cont as follows:
Next row (RS): Using 4mm (US 6) needle, *K2tog, rep from * to end.
25 (27: 29: 29: 31: 31) sts.
Beg with row 1, now work in patt as given for back and front as follows:
Work 5 rows, ending with a WS row.
Next row (RS): Using 4mm (US 6) needle, K3, M1, K to last 3 sts, M1, K3.
Working all sleeve increases as set by last row, inc 1 st at each end of 6th (6th: 8th: 8th: 8th: 6th) and every foll 6th (8th: 8th: 8th: 8th: 8th) row to 31 (45: 37: 45: 45: 51) sts, then on every foll 8th (-: 10th: 10th: 10th: -) row until there are 43 (-: 45: 47: 49: -) sts.
Cont straight until sleeve measures 44 (45: 46: 47: 48: 49) cm, ending with a WS row.

Shape top

Cast off 4 sts at beg of next 6 (4: 4: 4: 2: 2) rows, then – (5: 5: 5: 5: 5) sts at beg of foll - (2: 2: 2: 4: 4) rows.
Cast off rem 19 (19: 19: 21: 21: 23) sts **loosely**.

MAKING UP

Press all pieces with a warm iron over a damp cloth.
Join right shoulder seam using back stitch or mattress stitch if preferred.
Neckband
With RS facing, using 3mm (US 2/3) needles and yarn SINGLE, pick up and knit 30 (30: 30: 33: 33: 33) sts down left side of front neck, 58 sts from front, 30 (30: 30: 33: 33: 33) sts up right side of front neck, 30 (30: 30: 33: 33: 33) sts down right side of back neck, 58 sts from back, and 30 (30: 30: 33: 33: 33) sts up left side of back neck.
236 (236: 236: 248: 248: 248) sts.
Work in g st for 12 rows, ending with a **RS** row.
Join in second strand of yarn.
Using yarn DOUBLE, cast off knitwise (on **WS**).
Join left shoulder and neckband seam. Sew shaped cast-off edges of sleeves to back and front between markers denoting base of armhole openings.
Join side and sleeve seams, leaving side seams open below top of g st border.

ONE SHOULDER SWEATER

Pattern note: Garment is reversible.
Instructions given here are for garment with a right shoulder seam but garment can be worn either way round.

BACK
Work as given for back and front of wide neck sweater to **.
Cont straight until work measures 11 (12: 12: 13: 14: 15) cm **from markers**, ending with a WS row.

Shape back neck
Next row (RS): K24 (25: 27: 28: 30: 32) and turn, leaving rem sts on a holder.
Work each side of neck separately.
Cast off 3 sts at beg of next and foll alt row.
18 (19: 21: 22: 24: 26) sts.
Dec 1 st at neck edge of next 4 rows, then on foll 2 (2: 2: 3: 3: 3) alt rows.
12 (13: 15: 15: 17: 19) sts.
Work 2 rows, ending with a WS row.

Shape shoulder
Cast off 3 (3: 4: 4: 4: 5) sts at beg of next and foll alt row, then 3 (3: 3: 3: 4: 4) sts at beg of foll alt row **and at same time** dec 1 st at neck edge of 2nd row.
Work 1 row.
Cast off rem 2 (3: 3: 3: 4: 4) sts.
With RS facing, rejoin yarn DOUBLE, cast off centre 16 (17: 19: 19: 21: 23) sts **loosely**, K to end.
18 (18: 18: 19: 19: 19) sts.
Work 1 row.
Cast off 4 sts at beg of next and foll alt row, then 3 sts at beg of foll alt row.
7 (7: 7: 8: 8: 8) sts.
Dec 1 st at neck edge of next 4 rows, then on foll 1 (1: 1: 2: 2: 2) alt rows. 2 sts.
Work 1 row.
Next row (RS): K2tog and fasten off.

FRONT
Work as given for back and front of wide neck sweater to **.
Cont straight until work measures 11 (12: 12: 13: 14: 15) cm **from markers**, ending with a WS row.

Shape front neck
Next row (RS): K18 (18: 18: 19: 19: 19) and turn, leaving rem sts on a holder.
Work each side of neck separately.
Cast off 4 sts at beg of next and foll alt row, then 3 sts at beg of foll alt row.
7 (7: 7: 8: 8: 8) sts.
Work 1 row.

Dec 1 st at neck edge of next 4 rows, then on foll 1 (1: 1: 2: 2: 2) alt rows. 2 sts.
Work 1 row.
Next row (RS): K2tog and fasten off.
With RS facing, rejoin yarn DOUBLE, cast off centre 16 (17: 19: 19: 21: 23) sts **loosely**, K to end. 24 (25: 27: 28: 30: 32) sts.
Work 1 row.
Cast off 3 sts at beg of next and foll alt row.
18 (19: 21: 22: 24: 26) sts.
Dec 1 st at neck edge of next 4 rows, then on foll 2 (2: 2: 3: 3: 3) alt rows.
12 (13: 15: 15: 17: 19) sts.
Work 2 rows, ending with a RS row.

Shape shoulder
Cast off 3 (3: 4: 4: 4: 5) sts at beg of next and foll alt row, then 3 (3: 3: 3: 4: 4) sts at beg of foll alt row **and at same time** dec 1 st at neck edge of next row.
Cast off rem 2 (3: 3: 3: 4: 4) sts.

SLEEVES (both alike)
Work as given for sleeves of wide neck sweater.

MAKING UP
Press all pieces with a warm iron over a damp cloth.
Join right shoulder seam using back stitch or mattress stitch if preferred.

Neckband
With RS facing, using 3mm (US 2/3) needles and yarn SINGLE, pick up and knit 40 (40: 40: 43: 43: 43) sts down left side of front neck, 32 (34: 38: 38: 42: 46) sts from front, 46 (46: 46: 49: 49: 49) sts up right side of front neck, place marker on needle, pick up and knit 46 (46: 46: 49: 49: 49) sts down right side of back neck, 32 (34: 38: 38: 42: 46) sts from back, and 40 (40: 40: 43: 43: 43) sts up left side of back neck.
236 (240: 248: 260: 268: 276) sts.
Work in g st for 3 rows, ending with a WS row.
Next row (RS): K3, K2tog, K to within 5 sts of marker, K2tog tbl, K6 (marker is between centre 2 sts of these 6 sts), K2tog, K to last 5 sts, K2tog tbl, K3.
Rep last 4 rows twice more, ending with a **RS** row.
224 (228: 236: 248: 256: 264) sts.
Join in second strand of yarn.
Using yarn DOUBLE, cast off knitwise (on **WS**).
Join left shoulder seam of neckband **only**.
Sew shaped cast-off edges of sleeves to back and front between markers denoting base of armhole openings. Join side and sleeve seams, leaving side seams open below top of g st border.

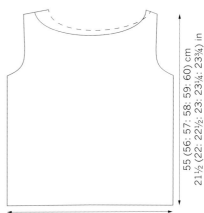

48.5 (50: 53.5: 55: 58.5: 61.5) cm
19 (20: 21: 22: 23: 24½) in

55 (56: 57: 58: 59: 60) cm
21½ (22: 22½: 23: 23¼: 23¾) in

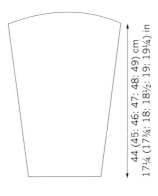

44 (45: 46: 47: 48: 49) cm
17¼ (17¾: 18: 18½: 19: 19¼) in

Recommendation ○○

Please see pages 50 & 51 for photographs.

	XS	S	M	L	XL	XXL	
To fit bust	**81**	**86**	**91**	**97**	**102**	**109**	**cm**
	32	34	36	38	40	43	in

Rowan Kidsilk Haze

A Steel

	3	3	3	4	4	4	x 25gm

B Shadow

	2	2	3	3	3	4	x 25gm

C Aura

	2	2	3	3	3	4	x 25gm

Needles

1 pair 3mm (no 11) (US 2/3) needles
1 pair 4mm (no 8) (US 6) needles
1 pair 8mm (no 0) (US 11) needles

Tension

12 sts and 19 rows to 10 cm measured over stocking stitch using a combination of 4mm (US 6) and 8mm (US 11) needles and yarn DOUBLE.

Special note: We found it preferable to knit the two yarns together from separate balls rather than winding them together.

DAZE
RELAXED RAGLAN SWEATER WORKED IN OMBRE STRIPES

STRIPE SEQUENCE
Rows 1 to 7: Using yarn A DOUBLE.
Rows 8 to 14: Using one strand each of yarns A and B.
Rows 15 to 21: Using yarn B DOUBLE.
Rows 22 to 28: Using one strand each of yarns B and C.
Rows 29 to 35: Using yarn C DOUBLE.
Rows 36 to 42: Using one strand each of yarns B and C.
Rows 43 to 49: Using yarn B DOUBLE.
Rows 50 to 56: Using one strand each of yarns A and B.
Rows 57 to 63: Using yarn A DOUBLE.
Rows 64 to 70: Using one strand each of yarns A and C.
Rows 71 to 77: Using yarn C DOUBLE.
Rows 78 to 84: Using one strand each of yarns A and C.
These 84 rows form stripe sequence and are repeated.

BACK
Cast on 119 (123: 131: 135: 143: 151) sts using 3mm (US 2/3) needles and yarn A DOUBLE.
Break off one strand of yarn and continue using SINGLE strand of yarn A as follows:
Row 1 (RS): K1 (3: 2: 4: 3: 2), *P2, K3, rep from * to last 3 (5: 4: 6: 5: 4) sts, P2, K1 (3: 2: 4: 3: 2).
Row 2: P1 (3: 2: 4: 3: 2), *K2, P3, rep from * to last 3 (5: 4: 6: 5: 4) sts, K2, P1 (3: 2: 4: 3: 2).
These 2 rows form rib.
Cont in rib until back measures 5 cm, ending with a WS row.
Join in second strand of yarn A.
Next row (RS): Using 4mm (US 6) needle and yarn A DOUBLE, K1, *K2tog, rep from * to end. 60 (62: 66: 68: 72: 76) sts.
Now work in patt as follows:
Row 1 (WS): Using 8mm (US 11) needle and yarn A DOUBLE, purl.
Row 2: Using 4mm (US 6) needle and yarn A DOUBLE, knit.
Last 2 rows form the patt, and last 3 rows form rows 1 to 3 of stripe sequence (see above).
Keeping stripe sequence and patt correct throughout as now set, cont as follows:
Work 59 (59: 61: 61: 61: 61) rows, ending

after stripe sequence row 62 (62: 64: 64: 64: 64) and with a WS row. (Back should measure approx 38 (38: 39: 39: 39: 39) cm.)
Shape raglan armholes
Keeping stripes and patt correct, cast off 3 sts at beg of next 2 rows.
54 (56: 60: 62: 66: 70) sts.
Work 2 (2: 2: 2: 2: 0) rows.
Next row (RS): K2, K2tog, K to last 4 sts, K2tog tbl, K2.
Working all raglan armhole decreases as set by last row, dec 1 st at each end of 4th (4th: 2nd: 4th: 2nd: 2nd) and 0 (1: 0: 0: 0: 0) foll 4th row, then on foll 13 (12: 15: 15: 17: 19) alt rows.
24 (26: 26: 28: 28: 28) sts.
Work 1 row, ending after stripe sequence row 14 (16: 18: 20: 22: 24) and with a WS row.
Cast off **loosely**.

FRONT
Work as given for back until 34 (36: 36: 40: 40: 40) sts rem in raglan armhole shaping.
Work 1 row, ending after stripe sequence row 4 (6: 8: 8: 10: 12) and with a WS row.
Shape front neck
Next row (RS): K2, K2tog, K5 (5: 5: 7: 7: 7) and turn, leaving rem sts on a holder.
8 (8: 8: 10: 10: 10) sts.
Work each side of neck separately.
Dec 1 st at neck edge of next 3 (3: 3: 4: 4: 4) rows **and at same time** dec 1 st at raglan armhole edge of 2nd and foll 0 (0: 0: 1: 1: 1) alt row. 4 sts.
Work 0 (0: 0: 1: 1: 1) row, ending with a WS row.
Next row (RS): K1, sl 1, K2tog, psso.
Next row: P2.
Next row: K2tog and fasten off.
With RS facing, rejoin yarns, cast off centre 16 (18: 18: 18: 18: 18) sts **loosely**, K to last 4 sts, K2tog tbl, K2. 8 (8: 8: 10: 10: 10) sts.
Complete to match first side, reversing shapings.

SLEEVES (both alike)
Cast on 51 (55: 59: 59: 63: 63) sts using 3mm (US 2/3) needles and yarn C DOUBLE.
Break off one strand of yarn and continue using SINGLE strand of yarn C as follows:

Row 1 (RS): K2 (0: 1: 1: 0: 0), P2 (1: 2: 2: 0: 0), *K3, P2, rep from * to last 2 (4: 1: 1: 3: 3) sts, K2 (3: 1: 1: 3: 3), P0 (1: 0: 0: 0: 0).
Row 2: P2 (0: 1: 1: 0: 0), K2 (1: 2: 2: 0: 0), *P3, K2, rep from * to last 2 (4: 1: 1: 3: 3) sts, P2 (3: 1: 1: 3: 3), K0 (1: 0: 0: 0: 0).
These 2 rows form rib.
Cont in rib until sleeve measures 7 cm, ending with a WS row.
Join in second strand of yarn C.
Next row (RS): Using 4mm (US 6) needle and yarn C DOUBLE, K1, *K2tog, rep from * to end. 26 (28: 30: 30: 32: 32) sts.
Now work in patt as follows:
Row 1 (WS): Using 8mm (US 11) needle and yarn C DOUBLE, purl.
Row 2: Using 4mm (US 6) needle and yarn C DOUBLE, K3, M1, K to last 3 sts, M1, K3.
Last 2 rows form the patt, last 3 rows form rows **71 to 73** of stripe sequence (see above) and last row sets increases for sleeve shaping.
Keeping stripe sequence and patt correct throughout as now set, working all sleeve increases as set by last row and beg with stripe sequence row **74**, cont as follows:
Inc 1 st at each end of 10th (10th: 12th: 10th: 10th: 8th) and 4 (4: 3: 3: 3: 1) foll 10th (10th: 12th: 10th: 10th: 8th) rows, then on 1 (1: 1: 2: 2: 5) foll 12th (12th: 14th: 12th: 12th: 10th) rows.
40 (42: 42: 44: 46: 48) sts.
Work 11 (11: 13: 11: 11: 9) rows, ending after stripe sequence row 62 (62: 64: 64: 64: 64) and with a WS row. (Sleeve should measure approx 47 (47: 48: 48: 48: 48) cm.)

Shape raglan
Keeping stripes and patt correct, cast off 3 sts at beg of next 2 rows.
34 (36: 36: 38: 40: 42) sts.
Work 4 (2: 2: 0: 0: 0) rows, ending with a WS row.
Working all raglan decreases in same way as raglan armhole decreases, dec 1 st at each end of next and 0 (0: 0: 0: 1: 2) foll alt rows, then on 6 (7: 7: 8: 8: 8) foll 4th rows. 20 sts.
Work 1 row, ending with a WS row.

Left sleeve only
Work 1 row, then cast off 6 sts at beg of foll row. 14 sts.
Dec 1 st at beg of next row, then cast off 6 sts at beg of foll row.

Right sleeve only
Cast off 6 sts at beg of next and foll alt row **and at same time** dec 1 st at end of 3rd of these rows.
Work 1 row.

Both sleeves
Cast off rem 7 sts **loosely.**

MAKING UP
Press all pieces with a warm iron over a damp cloth.
Join both front and right back raglan seams using back stitch or mattress stitch if preferred.

Neckband
With RS facing, using 3mm (US 2/3) needles and yarn A SINGLE, pick up and knit 36 sts from top of left sleeve, 12 (12: 12: 15: 15: 15) sts down left side of front neck, 33 (36: 36: 36: 36: 36) sts from front, 12 (12: 12: 15: 15: 15) sts up right side of front neck, 36 sts from top of right sleeve, and 49 (51: 51: 55: 55: 55) sts from back. 178 (183: 183: 193: 193: 193) sts.
Row 1 (WS): P3, *K2, P3, rep from * to end.
Row 2: K3, *P2, K3, rep from * to end.
Last 2 rows form rib.
Work in rib for a further 8 rows, ending with a **RS** row.
Join in second strand of yarn A.
Using yarn A DOUBLE, cast off in rib (on **WS**).
Join left back raglan and neckband seam. Join side and sleeve seams.

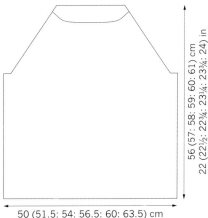

50 (51.5: 54: 56.5: 60: 63.5) cm
19¾ (20¼: 21¼: 22¼: 23½: 25) in

56 (57: 58: 59: 60: 61) cm
22 (22½: 22¾: 23¼: 23¾: 24) in

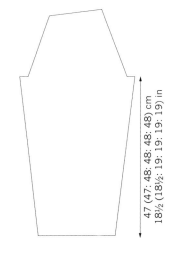

47 (47: 48: 48: 48: 48) cm
18½ (18½: 19: 19: 19: 19) in

INFORMATION

EXPERIENCE RATING

◯ for novice knitter
◯◯ for average knitter
◯◯◯ for experienced knitter

TENSION

Obtaining the correct tension is perhaps one of the most important factors which can make the difference between a successful garment and a disastrous one. It controls both the shape and size of an article, so any variations, however slight, can distort the finished garment. We recommend that you knit a square in pattern and/or stocking stitch (depending on the pattern instructions) of perhaps 5 – 10 more stitches and 5 – 10 more rows than those given in the tension note. Mark out the central 10cm square with pins. If you have too many stitches to 10cm try again using thicker needles, if you have too few stitches to 10cm try again using finer needles. Once you have achieved the correct tension your garment will be knitted to the measurements indicated in the size diagram shown at the end of the pattern. Please note, if you are unable to achieve the correct stitches and rows required, the stitches are more crucial as many patterns are knitted to length.

Keep an eye on your tension during knitting, especially if you're going back to work which has been put to one side for any length of time.

SIZING

The size diagram with each pattern will help you decide which size to knit. The instructions are given for the smallest size first, larger sizes follow in brackets. Where only one figure is given, this refers to all the sizes.

The measurements given on the size diagram are the actual size your garment should be when completed.

Measurements will vary from design to design because the necessary ease allowances have been made in each pattern to give your garment the correct fit, i.e. a loose fitting garment will be several cm wider than a neat fitted one, a snug fitting garment may have no ease at all.

CHART NOTE

Some of our patterns include a chart. Each square on a chart represent a stitch and each line of squares a row of knitting.

When working from a chart, unless otherwise stated, read odd rows (RS) from right to left and even rows (WS) from left to right. The key alongside each chart indicates how each stitch is worked.

FINISHING INSTRUCTIONS

It is the pressing and finishing which will transform your knitted pieces into a garment to be proud of.

Pressing

Darn in ends neatly along the selvage edge. Follow closely any special instructions given on the pattern or ball band and always take great care not to over press your work.

Block out your knitting on a pressing or ironing board, easing into shape, and unless otherwise states, press each piece using a warm iron over a damp cloth.

Tip: Attention should be given to ribs/edgings; if the garment is close fitting – steam the ribs gently so that the stitches fill out but stay elastic. Alternatively if the garment is to hang straight then steam out to the correct shape.

Tip: Take special care to press the selvages, as this will make sewing up both easier and neater.

CONSTRUCTION

Stitching together

When stitching the pieces together, remember to match areas of pattern very carefully where they meet. Use a stitch such as back stitch or mattress stitch for all main knitting seams and join all ribs and neckband with mattress stitch, unless otherwise stated.

Take extra care when stitching the edgings and collars around the back neck of a garment. They control the width of the back neck, and if too wide the garment will be ill fitting and drop off the shoulder.

Knit back neck edgings only to the length stated in the pattern, even stretching it slightly if for example, you are working in garter or horizontal rib stitch.

Stitch edgings/collars firmly into place using a back stitch seam, easing-in the back neck to fit the collar/edging rather than stretching the collar/edging to fit the back neck.

CARE INSTRUCTIONS

Yarns

Follow the care instructions printed on each individual ball band. Where different yarns are used in the same garment, follow the care instructions for the more delicate one.

Buttons

We recommend that buttons are removed if your garment is to be machine washed.

CROCHET

We are aware that crochet terminology varies from country to country. Please note we have used the English style in this publication.

Crochet abbreviations

ch	chain
ss	slip stitch
dc	double crochet
htr	half treble
dc2tog	dec by working 2 double crochet together
yoh	yarn over hook

Double crochet (dc)

1 Insert the hook into the work as indicated in the pattern, wrap the yarn over the hook and draw the yarn through the work only.

2 Wrap the yarn again and draw the yarn through both loops on the hook.

3 1 dc made.

Half treble (htr)

1 Wrap the yarn over the hook and insert the hook into the work as indicated in the pattern.

2 Wrap the yarn over the hook, draw through the work only and wrap the yarn again.

3 Draw through all 3 loops on the hook

Treble

1 Wrap the yarn over the hook and insert the hook into the work as indicated in the pattern.

2 Wrap the yarn over the hook draw through the work only and wrap the yarn again.

3 Draw through the first 2 loops only and wrap the yarn again.

4 Draw through the last 2 loops on the hook.

5 1 tr made.

dc2tog (dec)

1 Insert hook into next st, yoh, draw loop through twice, yoh.

2 Draw through all 3 loops on hook.

3 1 st decreased.

ABBREVIATIONS

K	knit
P	purl
K1b	knit 1 through back loop
st(s)	stitch(es)
inc	increas(e)(ing)
dec	decreas(e)(ing)
st st	stocking stitch (1 row K, 1 row P)
garter st	garter stitch (K every row)
beg	begin(ning)
foll	following
rem	remain(ing)
rev st st	reverse stocking stitch (1 row P, 1 row K)
rep	repeat
alt	alternate
cont	continue
patt	pattern
tog	together
mm	millimetres
cm	centimetres
in(s)	inch(es)
RS	right side
WS	wrong side
sl 1	slip one stitch
psso	pass slipped stitch over
tbl	through back of loop
M1	make one stitch by picking up horizontal loop before next stitch and knitting into back of it
M1p	make one stitch by picking up horizontal loop before next stitch and purling into back of it
yfwd	yarn forward (making a stitch)
yon	yarn over needle (making a stitch)
yrn	yarn round needle (making a stitch)-
Cn	cable needle next 2 sts onto a cn and hold at front of work, K2, K2 from cn.
-:	this dash indicates the particular instruction does not apply to your size

THANK YOU

We would like to say a big, big thank you to some amazing people without whom this book would not have been possible. Firstly, to our photographic team, Nicole for the fabulous photographs, Laura for the gorgeous hair & make-up and Freya our beautiful model, Lyndsay for the great graphic design, Sue and Tricia for their pattern writing & checking expertise and as always - Glenis, Margaret, Heather and Karan for all their wonderful knitting, Susan for her patience in finishing the garments, Richard & all at Lion, & finally to Neya, David, Sharon & all at Rowan for their ongoing support.

Kim, Kathleen & Lindsay

INDEX